List of Illustrations

Preface

to the Sixth Edition

Several years ago I attended a seminar during which the speaker went to great pains to point out the consequences of demographic change in the UK by the beginning of the 21st Century. We were potentially, he said, the first generation to find ourselves, our parents and our children living long enough to be lumped together as 'pensioners'. This startling fact revealed to us twenty years ago appears to have finally dawned on the powers-that-be, with the result there is now much talk of raising the pension age to 67 or even 70.

The last two decades too have been interesting times for businesses and organisations coming to terms with rapid developments in technology, economic trends and the increasing emphasis on the need to constantly review, adapt and restructure. Change during the last ten years has almost been elevated to the status of a virtue with layers of management and large numbers of manufacturing and some service industry jobs disappearing or being lost to the Indian sub-continent or the Far East.

There has also been a noticeable deterioration in employee satisfaction over the last decade. Despite legislation designed to prevent long hours and discrimination as well as guidance on good practice relating to stress at work, it seems the long hours culture and outdated attitudes are still prevalent in the workplace. So on the one hand there is pressure from the impact of a global economy affecting some sectors of employment, and on the other, the frustration of employees no longer satisfied with their working environment.

For all these reasons, career change is now a definite option to be considered. But changing direction can be like taking a leap into the dark: perilous and often frightening. But the

flipside to this is it gives you an unparalleled opportunity to wipe the slate clean and start again. For that reason alone you should give yourself a little space and time to take stock of your personal situation in detail and to get to know yourself better. If you do this, then you can start out on the road to your new career far more confident that you are heading in the right direction.

This book is to help you plan your voyage of self-discovery. It looks at who you are; what you are; what made you the way you are, and where you want to go to from here. It helps you evaluate your life skills both inside and outside the workplace; to put your personal circumstances into perspective; to recognise for yourself which careers you should concentrate on to suit you best; where to seek help if needed; how not to make the same mistakes again — if you made any before — and how to be realistic about what you ultimately want to achieve.

Provided you are well prepared, changing direction is not as daunting as it first appears: it can be exciting and challenging, offering you the golden opportunity of a new beginning.

On a personal note, my thanks to the members of the British Psychological Society who provided basic information for the original edition of this book, particularly Career Analysts, who at the time of Consultant Director George Summerfield, provided me with suitable case studies to illustrate discussion points; and Nick Williams who provided additional case studies on using hobbies as pointers to a successful career change.

Judith Johnstone

1

Moving On

REVIEWING YOUR SITUATION

The purpose of this chapter is to set you thinking about the
reasons why you are searching for a new career; what if anything
can be learnt from these, and what you need to know about
yourself before embarking on any new venture. This process
should not be rushed. STOP and THINK. Allow yourself the
mental space necessary to make the right decisions and to lay
solid foundations for a sound plan of action.

Your main difficulty may be to control the need you feel to do
something – anything – as soon as possible. Your sense of
urgency to escape an intolerable work environment, to pick
yourself up after an unexpected lay-off, or to satisfy your
frustration with your present career, can cloud your judgement. In
situations where change is forced on you, the pressure of family
and financial commitments may also be so great that worry leaves
you little room for careful reflection or sound planning.

In these situations there is always the temptation to throw
yourself at every available opening on offer, irrespective of
whether it is suitable or not. This 'scatter-gun' approach to the
job search can be totally counter-productive. How many times
do you hear stories about people who send out hundreds of job
applications but never make it to the shortlist? Their lack of
success does not necessarily illustrate how bad the jobs market is,
or how impossible it is to get employment even with experience
and good qualifications. The real lesson here is that ill-thought
out or rushed applications lead nowhere. No employer (or
financial backer if you are hoping to set up in business) is going
to give you a second glance if you are clearly unsuitable for the
job.

To succeed, you have to target your new career precisely. To
do this you must be confident you know where you are going,
and why. The answers to these questions are unique to you, and

1

the clues to help you unravel the mystery lie buried somewhere in your own personal history and the make-up of who you are.

HOW DID I GET HERE?

The world of work has changed dramatically over recent years. The workplace has altered out of all recognition. Computers and computerised systems are now the norm, not the exception. Communication is no longer limited to letters, telephones and fax machines. The impact of the Internet is everyhere. Communications and information technology skills have become paramount. There are few openings for those without them.

Organisational structures have also changed. Whole layers of management have been cut away. Multi-skilling is what is required of everyone. Flexibility is the name of the game. If you have only one string to your bow, your chances of employment are increasingly limited.

In the wider world, what happens to the global economy has a knock-on effect closer to home. Manufacturing is no longer a major player in the UK economy. The impact of the euro and the enlargement of the EU have yet to be evaluated over the longer term.

However, career change is not always forced on people by circumstances beyond their control. There are situations where individuals take matters into their own hands and decide to reshape their working lives themselves. This may be what you have decided to do.

Proactive change

Proactive change means taking the initiative yourself to start again. The 'trigger' might well be one of the following:

- **ambition** – aiming for a new career which will bring you better rewards (money, power, status etc) in the short or long run

- **self-development** – broadening the base of your skills to enhance and extend your choice of career in the future

- **second thoughts** – realising you are a square peg in a round hole and deciding to do something positive about it.

Reactive change

Reactive change is where change is imposed by external forces, such as:

- **redundancy, downsizing, delayering** – the job you were doing is no longer available, or your skills have become outdated

- **ill-health** – your employer feels unable to continue your employment because of your poor health record, or, if you have been self-employed, your business has been unable to carry on in your absence

- **dismissal** – your employment has been terminated for other reasons. (The manner and reason for your dismissal may affect what sort of job you can consider in the future.)

BEING IN CONTROL

This is all about proactive change, where you are making and taking the decisions yourself.

Changing employer

All of us at some time in our careers become disenchanted with the job we are doing. This is the employment equivalent of the 'seven year itch'. Boredom creeps in. Frustration at lack of promotion opportunities makes us resentful. There's no provision for training. The duties and responsibilities aren't what we expected. We feel undervalued or don't see eye to eye with the boss. The reasons can be many and varied.

Sometimes, it is possible to sort out your dissatisfaction by talking it through with the appropriate head of department and coming to an agreement on what should be done in future. For most people, however, the problem is often overcome by simply walking away from it, and seeking alternative employment with another organisation.

Changing direction

Changing your career as distinct from your employer has nothing to do with the 'seven year itch'. It is a fundamental

change. This is why you need to be absolutely clear about what you are doing, and why.

If you are in this situation, ask yourself *precisely* what it is that is making you want to leap into the unknown. Do you genuinely need a new career to reach the top, or just a change of work environment? Is there no way you can extend your skills by taking additional courses in your spare time? How do you know you are a square peg in a round hole? Saying so isn't enough.

Changing direction isn't an easy option: it requires your total commitment; almost always an element of retraining; the possibility of relocation, and a series of potentially crippling financial hurdles to cross. Throwing away a steady job – and your financial security along with it – is fine, as long as you are an independent, single person with no commitments. If you don't fit into this category, however, but are still resolutely determined to start again, then you need to be convinced you have *all* of the following:

1. **The wholehearted support of those who are dependent on you**. This does not mean announcing what you intend to do and demanding unquestioning loyalty regardless. Everyone who is directly affected by your decision must be fully aware of what is involved – and feel able to be supportive. This support could make all the difference between success and failure, so it should never be underestimated.

2. **A financial position solid enough to take the shocks of any unexpected set-backs**. You must be absolutely certain you are not in danger of having your home repossessed if your plans take longer to come to fruition than you anticipated, or that you are likely to reduce your nearest and dearest to a life-style bordering on poverty.

3. **The complete conviction that what you are doing is right, not just for you, but for everyone else who is close to you and affected by your decision**. This means not only being positive in your attitude, but also being realistic. You must be able to back up your assertions with hard, unassailable facts.

TAKING OVER CONTROL

If you are in the situation of having change forced on you, you need to find ways of moving from a sense of powerlessness to one of empowerment.

At first, frustration, anger and resentment have to be dealt with. Later, as the initial shock dies down, there can be bitterness or depression. Some people, however, experience a sense of relief once the axe has fallen. Employees in industries and commerce hardest hit by the effects of competitiveness in the global market place, or recurring recessions at home, have often seen the writing on the wall years before the cutbacks or closures begin. For some, the uncertainty of waiting for the inevitable can be harder to cope with than the event itself.

Once the job has gone, controlling what happens in the future passes back to you. The outlook may not be very bright, the opportunities limited, but at least *you* are now in the driving seat. *You* are taking an active part in the decision making process.

Why did I lose my job?

Before deciding what to do next, you need to clarify in your mind exactly why you lost your job, and if there is any way you could avoid this happening again.

Redundancy, downsizing, delayering
Although you might find it hard to appreciate the distinction, in a redundancy situation it is the *job* that is no longer required NOT necessarily the *person* who has been doing it.

Hiring and firing employees is an expensive undertaking. When a job becomes redundant, employers who have invested time and money in attracting good workers don't want to lose them if they can possibly avoid it. They would rather be able to offer alternative work within the organisation, or the chance of retraining if it is appropriate. It is only when these options are not available or the financial arguments are an overriding factor that the only course open to them is saying 'goodbye'.

There is no guarantee you will be able to protect yourself from being surplus to requirements again at some time in the

Can I avoid becoming surplus to requirements again?	
1. Was my work/time-keeping always up to the mark?	YES/NO
2. Were there areas I could have improved?	YES/NO
3. If YES, what were they?..	
4. Was I ever told to improve my work/ time-keeping?	YES/NO
5. Did I make any effort to do so?	YES/NO
6. If NO, why not?..	
7. Was there a good working relationship between me and my immediate boss?	YES/NO
8. If NO, why not?..	
9. Was I ever given the chance to take a training course to help me improve my work skills?	YES/NO
10. If YES, did I take it up?	YES/NO
11. If NO, why not?..	
12. If there was the chance to take up new ideas/work practices, was I enthusiastic?	YES/NO
13. If NO, why not?..	
14. Did I ever grumble about the introduction of new work practices?	YES/NO
15. If YES, did I show dissatisfaction?	YES/NO
16. Did I encourage other people to grumble?	YES/NO
17. If YES, was this noticed by my boss?	YES/NO
18. Did I actively show commitment to the organisation?	YES/NO
19. If NO, why not?..	
20. If I were the boss, would I employ me?	YES/NO

Fig. 1. Checklist: Can I avoid becoming surplus to requirements again?

future. However, there are some questions worth asking yourself
in case you unwittingly helped your last employer to decide you
should be included in the list of those who had to go. There is
no point in making yourself an unnecessarily easy target the
next time around.

Answer the questions set out opposite. If it helps, copy them
out and keep them by you as a constant reminder. Remember to
answer all the questions honestly. This exercise is for your own
use. You are not trying to impress anyone or make excuses.

If you tackle the questions honestly, your answers may
provide some clues as to why you and your last employer parted
company.

- Was your standard of work or time-keeping frequently
  questioned?

- Were you inflexible over adopting changes in work
  practices?

- Were you reluctant to take on board new technology or
  retraining?

- Were you seen as a trouble maker?

You may have good reasons and sound arguments to defend
yourself against such accusations, but it is worth pausing for a
moment and asking yourself if there was anything at all about
your attitude to work, or your superiors, which might have
reflected badly on you in the end. If you can spot anything
which might hint at this, then bear this in mind when you start
your next job, or you could be selecting yourself out of
employment once again at some time in the future.

Ill-health
A poor health record can lose you a job. There are limits to how
long an employer can stand the cost of your absence, whether
this is the occasional day off every week or so, or a long-term
illness lasting several months. It can also apply to situations
where your capacity to fulfil all your job requirements has
become impaired beyond the point where you can reasonably be

accommodated under the employment terms of the Disability Discrimination Act 1995.

If you lose a job through ill-health, make sure it is not your life-style that is contributing to the problem.

- Are you smoking or drinking too much?

- Are you an active sportsman or woman prone to frequent injury on the sportsfield?

- Is your diet what it should be?

- Are you taking enough exercise of the right sort?

- Are you taking drugs?

Employers can't be expected to be responsible for your health and safety outside the workplace. That responsibility has to lie with you.

Dismissal

Employment legislation ensures that employers wanting to remove an employee have to follow very precise procedures if they are not to be brought before an employment tribunal for unfair dismissal. Because of this, it should have been made very clear to you at some stage why you are being dismissed or asked to resign.

Dismissal because of your employer's dissatisfaction with some aspect of your work will make it harder for you to obtain a new job, particularly if you are expected to provide references which include your previous employer. So before tackling the job search, you will need to be very certain that whatever the cause of your dismissal, you will not allow yourself to become trapped by the same situation again.

WHY DO I WANT TO CHANGE MY CAREER?

Regardless of whether you are considering changing your career because circumstances have forced you to, or because you have taken the decision yourself, you need to be clear in your mind *why* you feel the change is necessary. This is important. On a

clean sheet of paper, write down a single statement why you *need* to make this change. This should help you focus more clearly on what you feel you should be aiming to achieve in the future. Keep this by you as you work through the various processes in this book.

LOOKING AT THE JOBS MARKET

In the first place, you have to decide whether you need to look for a new career in a totally new environment, or to concentrate on finding broadly similar employment with another organisation. Even if you want to stay in roughly the same type of work, circumstances may prevent you from doing so. There are three points to consider.

1. The restructuring of UK manufacturing and service industries.

2. The number of other people in the jobs market who can match your own level of skills and experience.

3. The current level of demand for people with broadly similar skills and experience.

The changing employment market

Was your previous employment in what has now become known as a 'contracting' industry? If it was, then looking for similar employment presents several problems.

*   Demand for workers across the whole sector will be declining.

*   There will be a large number of job seekers chasing a shrinking pool of jobs.

*   Getting another job in the same industry may not protect you from further cutbacks in future.

*   Starting with a new employer will leave you vulnerable to the 'last-in-first-out' principle if job cuts are being considered.

Employment trends

Even within the last few years, anyone in this position was being advised to monitor employment trends when planning their next job move. This way, it was argued, you could avoid or at least reduce the likelihood of future redundancy associated with contracting industries.

Unfortunately, the speed of change can upset the best laid plans. For instance, in this country since the end of World War Two we have seen the decline and collapse of many traditionally labour-intensive industries. Other industries have been lost to competition from abroad. Ship-building, coal-mining and steel-making for example, are now employing a tiny fraction of the workforce compared with the vast numbers they used to employ in the past. Here are very obvious examples of contracting industries. But whereas these changes took place over a number of years, and to some extent could be planned for, other shifts in economic activity have taken place over quite short periods of time.

In the late 1980s, the banking and financial sectors of the economy were booming. So were the sunrise industries of the new information technology. These were the 'expanding' job sectors many people were encouraged to target and retrain for. Within two years, however, the onset of a world recession and fluctuations in the UK's economic performance produced a marked reversal of this trend. Cutbacks and redundancies began to appear in job markets insulated against earlier downturns in the economy. Added to this, the rapid technological invasion of nearly every workplace in the last few years has continued to cut swathes through the numbers of employees on companies' payrolls. In the new millennium, the effects of the expansion of the EU, the Single Currency, and the impact of the global economy will no doubt reshape future employment trends. In the UK we are already seeing the unexpected demise of IT service industries unable to compete in the new highly competitive global marketplace. Other shocks may lie ahead which might have profound effects on our career expectations in years to come. The outsourcing of call-centre jobs to the Indian sub-continent and the rapid expansion of the Chinese economy are just two examples of sudden shifts in economic activity which no

one could have foreseen a few years ago.

Employment trends therefore are no longer as useful as they once were. They can only give a broad, general guide to future economic activity, *provided nothing unexpected or extraordinary takes place.*

The changing demand for skills

The days when you could find thousands of jobs involving semi-skilled or unskilled work have gone. Automation has replaced human labour and taken away great slices of activity which once involved mundane, routine tasks. Information technology is also beginning to take over in some areas of skilled and professional work, such as quality control and printing, design and administration. Transferable, or portable skills – skills which can be adapted and shaped to meet the requirements of several different types of job – are becoming increasingly important.

If your skills have become outdated in a shrinking market, you must be prepared to retrain if you are to succeed in finding new employment. Progress will not stand still simply to accommodate your need for a job, and there is no Divine Right to employment if you are not prepared to put some effort into it.

You may feel you are too old to learn new tricks. The simple truth is that thousands of people are doing exactly this throughout the country, and the opportunities for retraining or catching up with lost education are expanding all the time. Don't be put off by your age or use this as an excuse: you are never too old to learn – it might just take you a little longer.

Deciding to knuckle down to update or expand your skills is largely a matter of adopting the right attitude, but deciding precisely what skills should be updated or expanded has to be researched very thoroughly, and has a crucial part to play in your campaign to find the right career.

Where does this leave me?

If you know your hopes of getting back into your old type of employment are slim, this is the time to begin putting your future into sharper focus and to start planning with a clearer understanding of what you are trying to achieve. To do this you will need to build on your past.

PLANNING FOR THE FUTURE

Drawing your own self portrait

Looking closely at all aspects of your life up to now is a basic and essential part of the career planning process.

Over the next few chapters, you will be considering different aspects of your personal history, starting with your childhood, family and education. Other people should be involved at various stages of this exercise, such as your parents, siblings, colleagues, partners or children – in fact anyone who has played a major part in shaping who, and what, you are.

Other areas to be investigated will include:

- recognising your skills – in the widest sense

- recognising your strengths and weaknesses, and how to turn both of these to your advantage

- understanding your true motivational drives, and how these can be used to find a new career

- recognising the constraints on your freedom of action in choosing a new career – family, finance etc

- coming to terms with the options open to you.

Appreciating your achievements

To house all the details which will ultimately combine to illustrate your Self Portrait, you will need a few basic tools. At this stage it's better to get your information noted down as quickly as possible rather than going to a lot of trouble to produce an attractively finished piece of work. Remember your Self Portrait is a working document; it's for your benefit and no one else's. By all means spend time on this aspect later on when you have accumulated all the facts you need, but in the meantime all you need is:

- an A4 ring binder

- masses of scrap paper

- pens and pencils

- an A4 pad

- a robust folder to house any additional paper etc you may not want to punch holes in

- the willingness to spend time and effort on the project.

This last point is crucial. If you don't take the time and trouble to complete each step thoroughly, the end product will not provide you with the essential understanding you need to progress successfully.

At the end of the exercise, you may well discover you have an entirely new perspective on your life – not necessarily a very welcome one. Be prepared for this and for the need to make positive use of all your discoveries, however uncomfortable some of them may be.

As the years go by, a great deal of what we do and achieve fades from our memories: we forget our successes, or the reasons why we chose to do certain things at a particular time. The aim now is to lift these memories out of the attic, dust them off and scrutinise them, because somewhere in the past lie the clues waiting to act as pointers to the future.

CHECKLIST

- Have you a clear understanding why you are looking for a new career?

- Do you have the unqualified support of those dependent on you for the action you intend to take?

- Do you appreciate the reasons why you lost, or lost interest in, your previous line of work?

- Do these reasons tell you what situations you should avoid in future?

- Are your skills sufficiently in demand without needing to be updated?

- Are the numbers of people seeking employment within your field too great?

- Could you describe your skills as 'transferable' or 'portable'?

- Are the openings for these skills only in other industries which are showing signs of contracting?

- Are there any immediate problems you can identify which at the moment would make retraining difficult?

Before moving on to Chapter 2, record your progress against Milestones 1 and 2 in Appendix 1, page 137.

2

Who Am I?

PUTTING YOURSELF INTO CONTEXT

No matter how much fine detail you put into your Self Portrait, it will be incomplete unless you pay attention to filling in the background. To do this successfully, you need to reflect on several areas of your personal history – your:

- family background (parents and siblings)
- educational background and achievements
- personal development outside the education system
- personal preferences in educational subjects
- existing family composition (partner and children).

If you have a partner, encourage him or her to make the same journey into their own childhood. There are three good reasons why you should.

1. By being included in your voyage of discovery, your partner is being brought into the process of change at an early and often vital stage.
2. A partner's involvement can provide support and generate essential discussions which may help you keep a firm grasp on reality.
3. Your partner's previous life experiences might play a crucial role in helping you understand his or her point of view in deciding which future course of action would be best for everyone.

The process of involvement should also be extended to any other resident member of your household. This is particularly

important if your career change is likely to involve relocation to another part of the country.

Never forget that what you decide to do about your career could well have a profound effect on everyone around you, whether this person is an elderly relative living with you, or a child reaching a crucial stage in his or her education. You need to know as much about their individual goals and expectations as you do your own. It often takes something as cataclysmic as the enforced or even unenforced career change to highlight the diversity of interests and networks which have been carefully constructed by other members of the family while your attention was focused elsewhere. You ignore these factors at your peril.

YOUR CHILDHOOD FAMILY

Beginnings

The first two questionnaires in this chapter on pages 18 and 19 concentrate on the family you were born into and your place within it. As with all the questionnaires in this book, transfer the headings and the information you list under them onto A4 sheets to be incorporated into your binder as part of your Self Portrait.

Don't skip these questionnaires because you feel the information is irrelevant or unnecessary. Don't skimp on the details either. Your family circumstances when you were a child often have the greatest influence in shaping how you developed as a person, your subsequent outlook on life, and how you now respond to events and other people.

Try to use *all* the questionnaires you are asked to complete not just as fact-finding exercises, although this is important, but also as a basis for reflecting on your life experiences generally.

Now complete the questionnaire on pages 18 and 19.

Reviewing your family history

How much of these questionnaires were you able to complete without asking someone else to corroborate the factual information you needed? Does this tell you anything about your level of awareness of family influences? Is this perhaps an area you should give some thought to?

Sometimes the experience and skills of parents are taken for

granted as part of the world we grew up in. Often they get buried beneath the day-to-day demands of family life and remain unrecognised. The simple act of committing the information to paper can help to highlight not just the obvious areas of influence they had on our lives, such as tastes in music, literature or sport, but also the less obvious, such as what life experiences shaped their attitude towards education, work, self-improvement, personal relationships and so on. Delving deeper can be a revelation.

Is there anything in your parents' background which on reflection has affected your own attitude to life? Has this been a positive or negative influence? If this has been a negative input, consider how you might overcome this in future. If there is anything you believe to be important, note it down and keep it with the background questionnaire as part of your Self Portrait. Never discard any random thoughts or ideas. They are often of major importance.

Family traumas

Every family has its ups and downs. Disruption to the comparative calm of everyday life can come in many guises: a death in the family, divorce, remarriage, the arrival of step-children, relocation, the long-term hospitalisation of a parent, brother or sister, parental imprisonment or unemployment. These are just some possibilities that readily spring to mind.

In all probability your childhood will have experienced at least one of the above. Think about what they were. At the time, how aware of these traumas were you? Did any of them take place at a crucial time in your life, eg adolescence, or just before you were due to take an important examination? What effect did this have on you then, and why do you think you reacted in the way you did with the benefit of hindsight?

Personal traumas

These are likely to be those events which affected you directly. Consider the following:

* change of schools

The family I grew up in

                                    Father   Mother

Name
Date of birth
Place of birth
Religion
Schools attended

Qualifications gained

Date of marriage
Health
Hobbies/Social activities/
  community/war service

Details of previous marriage
  (if applicable)
Name of partner
Date of marriage
Details of children (names
  and date of birth)

How the marriage ended (death/divorce)
If your parents are no longer married give details . . . . .
. . . .
. . . .

Fig. 2. Self-assessment: Who am I?

Me

Full name ....

Pet name (if appropriate) ....

Date of birth ....

Place of birth ....

Religion ....

Details of brothers and sisters. (Put these in chronological order with date of birth and include yourself to show your position in the family order. Also indicate if any have died and the relevant date.)

1. ....

2. ....

3. ....

4. ....

Places where you spent your childhood and which you associate with most.

Describe relationships within the family unit (eg between parents, parents and children, children). Note anything you feel might be relevant.

- loss of a particular friend
- long-term personal ill-health
- the birth of younger siblings
- the age gap between you and your older/younger siblings
- changes in family relationships as you grew.

Other topics to consider
Here are further ideas to mull over. You will no doubt be able to think of others. Once again, don't disregard anything which now affects the way you look at the world, or your reaction to other people.

- **Were you aware of any family stresses as a child?** Have you since discovered you were shielded from these? If you were, what effect did discovering this have on you at the time of the discovery, and later, on reflection? If you were not shielded, how do you think this affected your own outlook on life?

- **Were there any personal pressures on you to succeed, or to take an adult role before you were ready to do so?** What effect did this have on you?

- **Did the name you were given benefit or hinder you?** Did it colour your behaviour? Would you have preferred to be called something else – and if so, what? What difference do you think it would have made to your life?

- **Have any of your childhood experiences made a lasting impression on you?** What are they and have they been beneficial or detrimental? Which was the most influential?

Summing up
Reflecting on your childhood and your role within the family at the time should provide you with the essentials of who you are and what influences shaped your early years. It should also identify those influences which outlasted childhood and continued to play a part in later years for better or worse. Begin

to consider how best you can use these influences now, or whether a shift in attitude might improve your chances of success in the future.

EDUCATION AND LEARNING EXPERIENCES

What have I achieved?

The questionnaire on pages 22 and 23 asks you to take a long and comprehensive look at not only your academic achievements, but also the wider learning processes accumulated over the passage of time. These are often either disregarded as irrelevant or underrated and need to be identified and appreciated for what they are – potentially useful life skills.

Don't consciously leave out any skills because you do not see yourself using them in the future. You might never envisage working as a personal assistant again, but shorthand can be a useful tool in many situations, and keyboard skills are increasingly in demand.

Don't overlook the everyday skills that can so often be taken for granted either, such as being able to drive. Leaving out anything can close the door on an option you may never have considered previously. Avoid prejudging the outcome and make sure you have included *everything*, however obscure it might seem.

Now complete the questionnaire on pages 22 and 23.

RECOGNISING YOUR ACHIEVEMENTS

You will almost certainly have a list of accomplishments which is longer than you anticipated when you began the exercise. This can be quite a boost to a deflated ego. As with the earlier questionnaire on your family background, much of what you achieved earlier in your life will have been submerged by later events. In your search for a new career, however, nothing must be wasted; everything can have a value. At this stage in the process, it is not always possible to see precisely what this value might be, but it is too early to discount anything. Note it. Keep

---

My education, training and achievements

Primary and Secondary Education

School   Dates   Achievements (including
                         prizes, badges, certificates,
                         qualifications, positions held
                         eg team member, member
                         of choir, club member-
                         ship, prefect etc).

Further Education and Professional Qualifications

Institution   Course   Qualifications and other
and Dates   taken   achievements (including
                         positions held, membership
                         of clubs etc).

Membership of Professional Bodies

Fig. 3. Personal achievements checklist.

Additional educational, training or vocational courses

(Include *any* course you have completed which is not covered by the earlier headings, including in-house training, non-academic examinations, those giving you licence to practice, or qualifications. Tick any you did for pleasure rather than out of necessity.)

Date	Course and course content	Exam result or qualification	Studied for pleasure

Of those studied for pleasure, which did you enjoy most and why?

Informal learning

List any skills you have acquired through practice rather than formal training, such as those arising from domestic responsibilities, eg counselling; care of the elderly, children, or the handicapped; gardening; decorating; car maintenance; a second language etc.

Areas which might need clarification

Your raw data in itself might not give a clear enough picture. For instance, if you took your examinations over several years then note down next to this information the reason why. Did illness prevent you taking them all at once? Did changing school mean a new syllabus? Did you have to sit some subjects as retakes? Did you get the unexpected opportunity to take an extra subject at a later date?

Think through the reasons why you took the subjects you did in the first place. Was it because:

- you liked them?

- you were good at them?

- your best friend was taking them?

- your parents wanted you to study them?

- they were essential entry requirements for the university/college course you wanted to follow?

If you went on to further or higher education, also ask yourself the following questions.

- Why did you decide to go on to further/higher education?

- Did you have a career firmly in mind?

- Did you see the course you chose as useful or essential?

Write down your answers to these questions once you are sure of them. The written word can be disarming: there can be no getting away from it, or pushing it out of your mind as you can with an unpalatable thought. Be perfectly honest, something you must be with all these questionnaires if they are to be of any help to you at all.

What your answers might tell you

Some people know from an early age that they want to follow one particular career. They have no qualms or second thoughts and go right ahead and achieve their objective. For most of us,

however, the decision is usually less straightforward.

At the time we are asked to make decisions about which subjects to continue and which we should drop, our life experiences are limited. Faced with thousands of possible careers to follow, we have insufficient information or appreciation about what many of these jobs involve. Nor do we have a sound basis for gauging our own future potential. Choices can be made for the flimsiest of reasons with no real understanding of where these might lead us, or more importantly, what career options we might be losing in the process.

Errors of judgement, however valid the reasons seemed to be at the time, can set us off on the wrong path for the rest of our lives – or until we are brought up short by redundancy or a mid-career crisis. If we build on shaky foundations, we shouldn't really be surprised if the construction is wobbly and finally comes tumbling down.

Looking at the reasons why you chose to study particular subjects at school may give you some idea why things did not work out so well later on. Similarly, if you went to college or university uncertain of what you wanted to do with your life at the end of two or three years, there's a good chance that the career you eventually chose was unsuitable.

Don't blame yourself unnecessarily if this is precisely what happened in your own case. Simply recognise that early decisions about what you wanted to do with your working life might have influenced not only your educational choices but also had a considerable part to play in reaching this stage in your career.

Case study: The danger of deciding too soon

At the tender and impressionable age of 8, Simon Capp made a firm decision to become a surgeon. This was entirely due to the experience of witnessing a road accident and his natural instinct of wanting to 'repair' the victim. This set the scene for all Simon's subsequent educational decisions and he worked hard to gain access to medical school and complete his training as a doctor.

Throughout all this time, however, Simon's main obsession

was in taking things to bits and repairing them, an obsession reflected in his hobbies. He was an incurable perfectionist and loved to work on the meticulous restoration and renovation of cars, houses and fine instruments. He was never happier than when he was immersed in these solitary, creative tasks.

Simon began to realise that 'repairing' people was not nearly so rewarding to him as repairing things. He recognised he would have been happier in engineering, but lack of mathematical ability prevented him from making the change. Increasingly, he found the stress and pressure of the medical profession too much for him. Combined with a disdain for the pushy style needed to become a consultant, he became increasingly unhappy and reached the point where he positively feared his patients. At 28 years of age, he badly needed a change, wanting most of all a career which reflected his hobbies. Interestingly, as a doctor he was best at practical procedures, such as those involved in chest strains, pleural taps and lumbar punctures.

Simon's motivational drives were all directed towards creative, practical crafts rather than science-based or welfare careers. Whilst he had a high level of intellect which had helped him to succeed in medicine, this was overridden by his interests and personality type. He needed to have an intellectual challenge and to be an expert, but had no urge to compete or climb the ladders of power. He was reserved, traditional and introspective with a need to be self-sufficient. He had little need to forge relationships, impress or connect with people generally. It was little wonder therefore that his time as a doctor had been one which induced in him a state of perpetual tension.

As his hobbies played such an important role in his life, Simon was encouraged to research the possibility of converting these into a full-time career, shifting his medical expertise into a part-time support role.

Simon discovered this was possible. He resigned and enrolled on a three year course in musical instrument making. To support himself, he continued part-time work in dermatology and family planning, but gave this up at the end of his course. By then, he had developed a specialist niche in reproducing medieval harps and 18th century baroque instruments for which there was a growing market. Using the old washroom of his cottage as a

workshop he could work in splendid isolation while bringing his work to a wider audience by exhibitions, presentations and lectures.

PERSONAL PREFERENCES IN EDUCATION

Likes and dislikes

How much of what we like or dislike depends on our personal experience, and how much is a reflection of conditioning by others? Very few of us are immune to other people's opinions, particularly as children. We grow up with examples of gender roles for example, or racial, religious and political attitudes, some of which may take years to overcome or rethink as the personal experience side of our lives comes increasingly into play.

The choice of subjects you studied, or the career you chose, may have been affected by parental or social expectations at the time, particularly in relation to what was, or was not, acceptable for a man or woman to do. Even today, in an age of equality of opportunity, gender stereotyping still exists.

Do you think this might have happened in your own case? What else might have influenced you?

To begin with make out five lists, each on a separate sheet of paper:

1. Those subjects you liked studying at school.
2. Those subjects you disliked studying at school.
3. Those subjects you found easy.
4. Those subjects you found difficult.
5. Those subjects you would have liked to study but were unable to.

Think carefully about the categories, or you may make the mistake of putting down subjects in List 1 which really belong to List 3. Just because you found music theory easy, does not necessarily mean you enjoyed doing it. Similarly, don't confuse disliking a subject with problems you had in mastering it.

Leave aside List 5 for the moment. Go through each of the first four lists in turn and ask yourself *why* the subject appears on the list it does. Here are some possible reasons:

- The lessons were good fun/boring.

- The teacher always picked on me.

- I always did well/badly at exams.

- I was good/bad at practical work.

- Everyone had to do it.

It may become clear to you that the reason you liked or disliked a particular subject had nothing to do with your ability or even your level of interest. Perhaps it had everything to do with the way the subject was taught or the relationship that existed between you and your teacher. Go through your list again if you can find instances of this and ask yourself if you might have felt differently about the subject if it had been taught by a different teacher at the time. Do you think this might have affected your choice of subjects studied in later years?

Lastly, return to List 5 and write down the reasons why you were unable to study this subject, and more importantly, why you wanted to study it in the first place. Later on in the discovery process, when considering which career path to follow in future, this may be a vital piece in the jigsaw.

YOUR FAMILY NOW

The last piece of work on your Self Portrait at this stage is to look at the composition of your present family, and the existing networks of those closest to you. Some of the information asked for in the questionnaire on pages 29 and 30 will have been provided already if your partner and other dependants have completed the earlier questionnaires with you, but there are residual questions which still need to be answered. Involvement of everyone who is capable of being involved is crucial to avoid inadvertently overlooking any aspect of someone's life which he or she regards as vitally important.

Complete this questionnaire now.

My family unit today

Partner

Name   . . . .

Date of birth   . . . .

Place of birth   . . . .

Religion   . . . .

Education

Secondary School College/University	Dates	Educational Achievements

---

Professional qualifications

Recent Career History

Job Title	Dates	Duties and Responsibilities

Hobbies, membership of clubs and leisure interests

Additional skills

Fig. 4. Family questionnaire.

Children (tick those still living at home)

Name   Date of birth   School, college,
                                      university or place
                                      of work

Hobbies, membership of clubs and leisure interests

Additional information (such as dates of important
examinations, health problems) . . . .

Other relatives living in your household
Name(s)

Relationship

Date(s) of birth

Religion(s)

Occupation(s) (if relevant)

Hobbies, membership of clubs, leisure interests

List all those who would have to move with you if you
relocated within the next twelve months.

Fig. 4. continued.

Considering the needs of your present family

A review of your family's connections and commitments at an early stage has the obvious advantage of giving you adequate warning of likely problem areas in future. The most obvious dangers are damaging a partner's career, or the examination chances of your children if you have to consider not just moving house, but relocating to another part of the country. It is pointless actively considering a post in the Outer Hebrides if you know the rest of your family has its roots going down to the bedrock of the Isle of Wight.

Financial pressures might force you to seriously consider such a drastic move, but before you do, you need to be sure there are no other options open to you. There is no mileage in pretending consultation doesn't matter. A family uprooted and dumped in what they regard as a 'hostile' environment may take months or even years to settle, if ever. The ultimate price of your autocratic decision may turn out to be an educational disaster for your children, a partner contemplating separation, or an elderly relative constantly pining for the loss of familiar faces and places. So take note of what you are told and appreciate there are others in the family unit with their own fears and uncertainties besides yourself.

CHECKLIST

- Have you completed all the questionnaires in this chapter honestly and to the best of your ability?

- Have you involved all those who should be consulted?

- Were there any details about your childhood that you had not been aware of up to this time?

- If so, do these make any material difference to your outlook on life?

- Have you discovered anything about your decisions to study particular subjects either at school or at college which you feel might be relevant to your current difficulties?

- If so, do you feel these are important enough to be taken into consideration when looking for a new career?

- Have you discovered anything about your partner's accomplishments/commitments you were unaware of until this exercise?

- If so, do you appreciate what the significance of these might be in relation to your efforts to start a new career?

- Have you discovered anything about your children's lives or those of any other dependent relative living with you that will also affect the way you approach your career search?

- If so, are you prepared to accommodate their expectations within the planning stage of your career search?

Before moving on to Chapter 3, record your progress against Milestones 3–8 in Appendix 1, page 137.

3

Drawing on Work Experience

The next part of your Self Portrait is looking in depth at your work experience. This means not just *what* jobs you did, but *why* you did them; what you liked or disliked about them; what you think you might like to do in the future; and finally, what might prevent you from making your dreams become a reality.

WHAT JOBS HAVE I DONE?

The questionnaire on page 34 should be completed now. This will be the working document you will use as a reference point for the remainder of the chapter.

You will see that you are asked to work forward in time rather than the reverse. There is a sound reason for this. The questionnaire is not meant to be an application form or a curriculum vitae. Both of these nowadays place greater emphasis on the last position held and give less prominence to earlier employment. The questionnaire however, is meant to do the opposite; to take you through your career history from its earliest, perhaps humble beginnings, and by doing so to help you examine your reasons for moving on to the next job. Make the record as comprehensive as possible. Include your very first paper round if necessary, and any periods of work experience for which you did not get paid.

ANALYSING YOUR WORK HISTORY

Type of jobs

Your list may give you a very clear picture of the type of job you have always gone for, such as teaching, administrative, marketing, physically demanding, computing etc. If there is no consistency in your pattern of *type*, is there any consistency of work environment which could be seen as a pattern? For

---

My working history and experience

(Start with your very first job and work forwards in time. Also include any periods of employment or work experience for which you did not get paid, and any part-time or temporary employment.)

Dates	Job title and name of employer	Duties and responsibilities	Reason for leaving

Fig. 5. Working history and experience.

instance, were you desk-bound or mobile, indoors or outdoors? Were you working in isolation or as part of a team? Were you one of many, or one of a few?

Patterns are important when considering what action to take in future. You may have had a marked preference for a particular working environment. Conversely, you may have had a marked loathing for it too. Which was it? Think about this carefully. Make notes of anything which you feel is relevant or important.

Duties and responsibilities

What happened to the level of duties and responsibilities you undertook over the years? Did they increase rapidly during your early years of employment and then flatten out as time went by, or was there a steady increase over the whole period? Whichever is true, were you happy with this state of affairs, or would you have liked to see a different pattern if you had had the choice?

Looking ahead, consider what level you would ultimately like to work at in your new career. Do you want more responsibility, less or roughly the same? Make a note of what you decide.

Looking at your first job in detail

For this part of the exercise it is important to consider your first full-time, fully paid employment.

Why did you choose this particular job? Write down your answer and consider the implications. State precisely *why* you wanted the job in preference to any other. Here are some possibilities:

- It sounded interesting.

- The money was good.

- My best friend was working with the same company.

- They were recruiting art graduates.

- The training programme was good.

- If you worked hard you could get promotion quickly.

- It was the only job going at the time.

- I couldn't think of anything else.

- My father/mother/parents wanted me to take it.

Like picking subjects to study at school, any of the above reasons may have been perfectly valid at the time, but with hindsight some of them are hardly the stuff on which to build solid foundations for a future career. Ask yourself what effect this first choice had on the rest of your career. Was it a mistake? Did you recognise it and change course or did you just plough on regardless and make the best of a bad job? If you had your time over again, would you make the same choice – and why? Once again, write down your thoughts so that nothing is overlooked later.

Case study: Educating yourself into a cul-de-sac

Susan French (31) obtained a degree specialising in Scandinavian languages and went on to gain additional secretarial qualifications and Teaching English as a Foreign Language. After qualifying, she automatically chose office work as a natural consequence of her studies and obtained numerous secretarial jobs through an agency.

However, she was never completely at ease in her secretarial role. What she enjoyed most was helping out at a children's home in her spare time, particularly with the craft work and she began to question whether or not she had chosen the right direction for her career.

Her dissatisfaction with her choice of work increased until she decided to seek professional careers advice to give her some much needed guidance.

Her assessment results showed that she was highly motivated towards welfare or caring careers but with the additional need for academic work.

These findings reinforced what Susan herself already knew at heart, that she would only be happy working with people and that she had the academic ability to tackle whatever job she set her mind to.

With this in mind, she took a job as a 'helper' in an

Occupational Therapy Department with the intention of moving up the promotional ladder to a higher grade.

The pros and cons of each job

Every job has its good and bad points. The next part of the exercise is to work your way through all the jobs on your questionnaire, including the casual, temporary or part-time ones you have listed.

Take yourself back to the time you were doing that particular job. Remember the work environment, the people you worked with and those you worked under. Remind yourself of what was involved in the day-to-day duties and responsibilities of the job itself. Take this further and reflect on the whole period you were employed on this job. Did it work out the way you expected when you started? Did anything happen which affected your attitude towards the job later on? Was this good or bad? Did it ultimately make you decide you wanted to look elsewhere for new employment?

Having refreshed your memory about the job, now make two lists under the headings 'Likes' and 'Dislikes'. The following list is a rough guide to areas of the job which could be usefully analysed. You can add others which might be relevant in your own case.

- **Aspects of the job content**. Identify specific duties you liked or disliked.

- **Level of responsibility**. State why you liked or disliked the level of responsibility attached to the post.

- **Work environment**. Restrict your comments to the place rather than the people.

- **Colleagues**. Divide this group into three: subordinates, peer group and bosses. Put names to the people you list and say why you liked or disliked them.

- **Pay structure**. State what was good or bad about it.

- **Hours of work.** State your reasons for liking or disliking the system you had to work.

- **Holidays**. Was there anything about the conditions under which you had to take your holidays which were good or bad as far as you were concerned?

Finally, write down what you liked *most* about the job, and what you liked *least*.

Complete this exercise for every job individually *using the same headings* and compare your notes.

What do these lists tell me?
Both lists have their uses, so don't just concentrate on the 'Likes' and forget about the 'Dislikes'.

The list of 'Likes' should give you a rough idea what gives you the most satisfaction from any job. Identifying the one aspect of the job you liked most is also a pointer to what you should be looking for in future. *But this is only a pointer.* What you liked most might be nothing more than the best of an indifferent set of circumstances rather than an essential requirement of any future career.

The list of 'Dislikes' should be used as a warning to remind you of aspects of past jobs you found irksome, or worse. Take note of these and weigh up their importance, or their significance. Pay attention to the aspect you liked least because once again this is a pointer. It tells you clearly what you should avoid in future if possible.

Where your greatest 'Like' or 'Dislike' involved colleagues, this means you are more likely to place greater store on working relationships than the content of the work itself, or the environment in which it takes place. Interpersonal chemistry is a mysterious human process and is something which unfortunately is often impossible to evaluate until you start a job. The only exception to this is when you are interviewed by your potential boss and you know immediately there is something about him or her which would set your teeth on edge if you had to work with them.

Which job did I enjoy most?
Looking through your job list, select one job taken all round you enjoyed the most. Include in your consideration the

complete job list on your questionnaire and not just the full-time paid positions you have held.

Don't be put off selecting one of the casual or temporary posts: in this exercise, every post has to be given equal consideration as the next. If you find yourself choosing one of these 'lesser' posts, you have signalled there was something about the job which was important and needs to be recognised when planning your future career. Equally, in making your choice, don't automatically pick your last job. It may represent the pinnacle of your career so far, but it may not represent the one which gave you the most personal satisfaction.

When you have decided, write down your choice and say why, when you look back over your career history, this job means more to you than all the rest. Think over the implications of what you have written. Are there any surprises? Have you finally revealed something to yourself you have been hiding away for years?

LOOKING AHEAD

What would I like to do in the future?

Having concentrated on the past, it is now time to let your imagination run riot and think about the future. This part of the exercise is all about what you *want* to do, not what you *can* do.

Commit your thoughts to paper. Be honest with yourself and don't rule out anything on the grounds that it sounds silly, or too outlandish. At this stage, anything goes, from flights of pure fantasy to cherished notions you have held for years but have never dared admit to. Remember, if your Self Portrait is to reflect a true likeness of yourself, you can't afford to cheat on details.

What happens if you can't identify a particular career immediately? Don't worry. In fact, trying to pin yourself down to any particular career at this stage might well be too restricting. Adopt the broad brush approach if this helps, using all-embracing ideas such as:

I want to look after animals.
I don't want to be stuck in an office.

I want to travel.
I'd like to help people.
I want to control my own working day.
I want to be creative.

Put down as many ideas as possible, expanding on the one before if you can to begin the process of fine-tuning the original thought. Start to put your ideas into a working environment.

For instance, take the first example – 'I want to look after animals.' Think about in what context.

- Do you want to care for them when they are sick?

- Have you any particular type of animals in mind?

- Do you want to rear them?

- Do you want to look after them on a nine-to-five basis or at any time?

- Do you want to be part of a conservation or animal welfare group?

- Would you want to work indoors, outdoors or a bit of both?

From these answers, a whole range of potential career openings begin to emerge.

- Veterinary surgeon or nurse.

- Groom, stable or kennel hand.

- Zoo keeper.

- Farmer, stockman or shepherd.

- Fish farmer.

- Ranger or conservationist.

- Butcher.

- RSPCA Inspector.

- Animal charity worker.

As you can see, the range of possibilities is surprisingly large. It can range from the humble to the exalted, the practical to the theoretical, the office-based to the outdoor, the national to the international.

Let yourself go. Brainstorm if necessary, and see what you have got hidden away in the inner recesses of your mind that you haven't dared admit to yourself until now. Write it all down on paper: it can't escape your grasp if you do. It's there, a tantalising glimpse of a possible future.

At the end of the exercise you may still not be able to pin down precisely what you want to do. You may only have a very rough idea what you want from the world of work. Don't worry, the next chapter will help to fill in more of the detail you need to complete your picture.

If you have a very firm idea of what career you want to follow, however – it may have been your deepest wish ever since you left school but circumstances prevented you from following it up – admit to it. Say it. Write it down. 'I want to be a . . . '.

Now, what's stopping you?

What is stopping me?

This is where reality creeps in. This is the point where your feet have to be firmly rooted to the ground. It does not necessarily mean your goal becomes unattainable, it may just have to be achieved over a longer period of time or by a more circuitous route, but it has to be recognised there are situations which make it impossible or difficult for you to achieve your aim.

Unrealistic targets

There are quite obviously some careers which are forever closed to us if we lack the basic essential talent for them, have physical limitations or are hampered by the times we live in.

No amount of wanting to become a famous violinist will be of any use if, despite endless practice and tuition, you fail to master the instrument. Nor is there any point in hankering after becoming a fire fighter if you have defective vision or a physique which does not come up to the required standards.

Equally as futile is the longing to be involved in the terraforming of Mars: you can do nothing except resign yourself to the simple fact that you have been born too soon.

Wrong qualifications
This is a problem which usually dates back to decisions we made in our mid-teens about which subjects we were good at and should keep studying, and which subjects we were bad at and should drop.

This simplistic approach can be very persuasive. Subjects get dropped which might prove vital to your career prospects in later life. You would have been better advised to keep as broad a mix of subjects as the curriculum would allow and offered extra tuition in those you found difficult.

If you are faced with a situation where your qualifications, or lack of them, is likely to bar your progress, there is no need to despair. Every year, thousands of people start from scratch to make up the deficiencies of their earlier education. There is a stunning array of the provision available for the mature student, with or without relevant qualifications. Only in circumstances where the time taken to qualify is long-term, and the number of years available to you to practise your new career before retirement is limited, are there any upper age barriers to block your way.

Writing to the professional body of the career which interests you will also produce information, not only on what entry qualifications will be required, but any additional study which might be expected if you are to gain full professional status.

Inadequate skills or experience
This too is not necessarily an insurmountable problem. If you are considering going back to study, periods of work experience in sandwich courses or additional work taken on during the vacation periods may well be sufficient to give you an acceptable grounding.

Personal approaches to businesses or organisations in the field you are interested in may also provide you with suggestions on how to gain additional skills or experience.

If you live in England, you may find it useful to contact your local Learning and Skills Council (LSC) who have the responsibility for the post-16 and adult learning initiatives. The LSC for your area will be listed in *The Phone Book* or you will find them through the national website www.lsc.gov.uk.

If you live in Wales, contact The National Assembly for Wales on (029) 2082 5111 to find what initiatives are currently available. You can also find information on www.wales.gov.uk. In Northern Ireland, contact the Department for Employment and Learning on (028) 9025 7777 or access their website www.delni.gov.uk.

In Scotland, the initiatives have been delegated to the Scottish Executive Education and Training Department on 08457 741741 or www.scotland.gov.uk.

Getting involved with voluntary work in the area which interests you is also a good way of making up lost ground, particularly in caring roles.

Too old
Legislation aimed at dealing with age discrimination in employment will not be implemented before 2006. However, many employers are already coming to realise older, more mature employees appeal to the growing number of older, more mature customers.

In most cases, age has nothing to do with making a fresh start. It can of course limit the amount of time you have available to reach the top, but if reaching the top is not your aim, then don't persuade yourself this is an adequate reason. As the Open University roll of students amply demonstrates, you are never too old to learn – it might just take you a little longer.

Lack of confidence
If you have been employed by a single organisation all your working life, or in the same type of work, starting out into the unknown can be a daunting prospect. The experience of losing a job and the self-doubt that accompanies this can strangle your sense of adventure, consciously or unconsciously. There is a terrible tendency to talk yourself down, or to concentrate on the negative side of life. This not only puts off prospective

employers and friends, it has a debilitating effect on your own mental well-being.

There is no easy answer to this problem except trying to adopt a more positive approach to your new job search, secure in the knowledge that you are doing the right thing both for yourself and your family. Being sure is the hard part, which is why you are about the business of unravelling your past to build a more solid future.

Family or other commitments
These are genuine difficulties which have to be considered in detail. For instance, it is no good glossing over the problems of being a full-time or even a part-time student if you have young children. You may:

- miss out on crucial periods of their development

- be placing too great a burden on your partner in confining the caring role to one person

- jeopardise his or her career in the process.

In other words, you may be storing up stresses and strains which will ultimately lead to family breakdown or divorce.

Other commitments can be equally demanding eg:

- the weekly meeting of the youth club you are running

- the number of days you are obliged to sit as a magistrate

- your regular session recording the local paper onto tapes for the blind.

Whatever your commitments, evaluate each one carefully and aim to retain your links with only those you believe are vital. For those which have to take a back seat for a while, explain the reasons for your temporary unavailability and keep in touch. Don't be tempted to drop them completely. Any network of contacts and connections you have built up in the past might prove valuable in the future.

Finance
Combined with the difficulties you are likely to encounter with family and other commitments, financing yourself and your dependants through a period of change can sometimes be the main obstacle to retraining or starting afresh. Having to finance your own period of study can be a harrowing experience.

Because this is a topic which needs looking at in detail, the whole of Chapter 9 is devoted to it.

Attitude
Don't let your approach to a new career be dogged by a negative attitude or excuses which boil down to simply not wanting to put yourself out to make the effort. If you aren't prepared to put anything into your search for a new beginning, then you can't expect to get anything worthwhile out of it at the end.

CHECKLIST

- Have you taken care to include *all* your work experience in the questionnaire?

- Have you identified a pattern in the type of work you have done previously?

- Have you been able to clarify your reasons for taking your first full-time permanent job? If so, with hindsight are you satisfied it was the right choice?

- What have you discovered about your 'likes' and 'dislikes' in the various jobs you have had over the years?

- Does this knowledge give you any clear pointers which you should take into account when considering a new career?

- Which were the factors you considered to be most important when you picked out the job you enjoyed most?

- What ideas for possible future careers have you generated from your brainstorming session?

- What obstacles have you identified which might prevent you following any of these as a career?

- What measures can you take, if any, to overcome these problems?

- Are the obstacles genuine, or simply excuses for inaction?

Before moving on to Chapter 4, record your progress against Milestones 9–17 in Appendix 1, pages 137–138.

4

Building on Hobbies and Interests

DISCOVERING YOUR MOTIVATION

Why this is so important

What you do in your spare time is a far better indicator of the type of working environment you prefer than your career history. Why is this?

The answer is simple – you take up a hobby or an interest because you *want* to, not because you *have* to. Perhaps when you were younger, and your parents did your thinking for you, they decided it would be a good idea if you joined the Brownies/Cubs, or went to ballet classes or football training. Once you were old enough to have your own say in the matter however, your personal choices took over from parental ones. They may have been similar; they may have been completely different; but the big difference was they were *your own*.

The motivation behind your decision to spend time doing one thing rather than another is unique to you: you are motivated to do something because you enjoy what you are doing, and you enjoy doing it because it fits in very precisely with your own preferences. If it didn't, you would stop doing it and take up something else.

Looking for the right career means identifying these motivational drives, understanding their significance and transferring them to the workplace.

Case study: Trying to be someone you're not

Amy Howard was 26. Her main hobby was gardening. She loved it. Despite having lots of other hobbies, gardening and garden design had played a very large part in her life, but she had never felt confident enough to pursue the idea that she could make a career out of it.

Amy was the child of academic parents. She went to university and gained a BA in English. Subsequently she had a

succession of jobs, primarily as a hostel worker for homeless young people. Wanting a change to something more creative she resigned and joined a theatre company, also attending evening classes in art, pottery, screen printing and writing.

As time passed, the need for financial security became increasingly important to her and her initial reaction was to turn again to community work. Her attempts to get back into this type of employment, however, met with no success and she began to wonder if she might not be better trying her hand at something completely different.

Amy's motivational drives confirmed her main interests lay in practical rather than caring careers. She had been a successful social worker only because she was capable of being calm in a crisis. However, she had fared less well when needing to be assertive.

It was clear Amy had a strong liking for working with tools and materials and producing tangible results. She also had a need for artistic expression. Combined with indications that she would be able to cope with self-employment, everything pointed towards her making the most of one of her hobbies, in this case either pottery or gardening.

Amy was encouraged to consider several options, including courses in agriculture and horticulture. Two years later she had started up her own gardening and garden design and construction business, and was also involved in teaching the subject at adult education classes.

INDENTIFYING EARLY INTERESTS

Influence during your school years

Although some of your earlier interests might have been parent or teacher inspired, not all of them will necessarily have been discarded in later life. Interests kindled during childhood can expand and develop with the passing years into related hobbies, or become springboards into others. For this reason it is important to take them into account to appreciate the development which might have taken place, and what signposts they may offer from an employment point of view.

When you complete Part I of the questionnaire opposite

Hobbies and interests			
Part I – Childhood **Age 4–11 years**			
Subject/Club Society	What was involved and achievements	Age when discontinued	Reason for discontinuing
Age 12–18 years			
Subject/Club Society	What was involved and achievements	Age when discontinued	Reasons for discontinuing
Part II – Membership of clubs and associations since leaving school			
Dates	Name of club/society/ association	Official roles	Reason for discontinuing

Fig. 6. Hobbies and interests list.

put in as much detail as possible. Include membership of clubs or societies and any status or merit achieved, such as captain of a team, school team member, badges obtained, trophies won, first violin etc. Here you have the basis for the interests you developed in later years.

Before moving on to Part II, identify the hobbies or interests you enjoyed most. Did you have a particular favourite? What was it? Are you still involved with this interest in some way? Are there any you regret giving up? Would you like to take them up again if the opportunity presented itself? As always, write down the answers for future reference.

Identifying later interests

Membership of clubs and associations since leaving school
List your later affiliations in date order in Part II of the questionnaire. Highlight any official roles you held, and for how long. Also include in this section any formal or informal groups you joined with your colleagues, on or off work premises which were social in nature, such as a darts or quiz team, a rambling group or social club.

As you did with Part I, look through the later list of activities. Once again, was there any interest which was a clear favourite, and why? Do you regret having given anything up? Is there anything preventing you from taking it up again now or in the future?

Recognising personal initiatives

Self-motivation is a powerful force. Harnessed to a particular goal or project, it can achieve wonders. It is particularly useful in a situation where you are aiming to achieve something new and where your success is likely to depend on your personal level of drive and determination.

Bearing this in mind, at any stage in your life did you ever take it upon yourself to organise or initiate an event of any description? If you did, make a separate list of these. It doesn't matter how young you were at the time, or how trivial it might seem now on reflection. It might have been something as simple

as raising money for a charity collection at school, or putting on a puppet play to entertain your friends. Add it to your list. The fact that you initiated it is what counts.

In compiling your list of personal initiatives, work forward from your school days up to the present time. Include anything which might be connected with the social side of your employment, such as departmental quiz teams, firms' dances or staff magazines. Don't, however, include anything which directly relates to work practices themselves. The motivation for initiating action in the workplace is often triggered by other influences, such as a company's expectations of its employees or a generous bonus payments system. If you had had exactly the same job with a different employer, you might never have had the necessary stimulus to generate the idea, so include only those activities which were self-motivated.

As you make your list, write down what part you played and whether it changed. Did your role remain solitary, or did you delegate and become part of a team? Is there a pattern in how you handle your initiatives? Both the initiative and your way of building on it are good indicators of how you like to work.

YOUR MAIN INTERESTS NOW

What you enjoy doing most in your spare time

Moving on to your present interests, stick to those which you can honestly say are of real interest to you. Don't include activities which have been allowed to slip over the years, or those you participate in so infrequently they really cannot be said to play a major part in your life. Use as a guideline a regular commitment of your time on a daily, weekly or monthly basis.

The next questionnaire on your interests on page 54 has been divided into three parts:

- hobbies

- leisure pursuits

- voluntary work/commitments.

For the purposes of this exercise, it is useful to make a clear distinction between these three headings. Understand what these distinctions are before you complete the questionnaire.

Why the distinction?

Hobbies and leisure pursuits are terms which are often confused. They are, however, quite distinct and for the purpose of this exercise this distinction should be recognised for the following reasons:

1. To identify your additional skills or specialised knowledge which could be built on to provide a new career.

2. To separate the very different motivational drives behind your choice of spare time activities which need to be taken into account.

Hobbies

Hobbies are activities: they are pastimes in which the stimulus is from within yourself. You play squash or swim. You are a do-it-yourself addict or cook. You collect stamps or raise gardenias. You write fiction or paint watercolours. You are motivated to do something.

Hobbies usually require a *skill* of some sort or *specialised knowledge*. This skill or knowledge may only be minimal, or it may be on a par with that of an expert; it may have been acquired by watching others, by personal trial and error, by practice or by taking lessons – but you have been motivated to acquire it, which is why it is special.

Leisure pursuits

Leisure pursuits are precisely that: the pursuit of leisure. They are pastimes in which you have no active part to play: someone else is providing the stimulus. You watch television or listen to music. You go to the theatre or the cinema. You are a football supporter or avid reader of fiction.

Your motivation in these situations is quite different. You are seeking the opportunity to sink yourself into another world for a while – to take a break. You are a spectator. It is not essential to

have a basic skill or specialised knowledge. You can enjoy the experience for its own sake.

Voluntary work or commitments
Your level of motivation to do unpaid work within the community is another useful guide to your personality and preferences. Like your hobbies, it demands activity on your part, but this time the direct benefit is felt by others and not yourself. You may have the indirect benefit of getting personal satisfaction from doing the work, but this is only because it has given pleasure, or helped to make somebody's life a little easier. There has to be feedback from someone else.

Community work might involve a local branch of a national charity, or a group which has sprung up from within the community itself to meet a particular need. Or it may be a personal commitment you have taken on board which is not the responsibility of any organised group, such as regular shopping for an elderly neighbour, providing transport to and from hospital etc.

Completing the questionnaire
When listing the skills or specialist knowledge involved in a particular hobby, or in community roles, make this as comprehensive as possible, including physical skills. For example –

tennis:

- fast reflexes

- good eye/hand co-ordination

- controlled arm movement

- an understanding of the rules of the game

- strategy

- stamina

- an appreciation of team work (doubles).

My spare time interests today			
Hobbies			
Hobby	Duration of interest	Time spent per week etc	Skills or specialist knowledge needed
Leisure pursuits			
Leisure pursuit	Duration of interest	Time spent per week etc	Reason for interest
Voluntary work or commitment			
Type of work and name of organisation	Duration of interest	Time spent per week etc	Skills or specialised knowledge needed

Fig. 7. Current spare time interests.

secretary of a local charity:

- good administration (minute taking, letter writing, committee organisation, working to deadlines, methodical)
- office skills (shorthand/typing, word processing, use of IT systems and telephone, keeping filing system)
- social skills (good listener, good communicator, diplomatic)
- able to work unsupervised
- able to work as part of a team.

As you can see from the above examples, you probably possess many more skills and far more knowledge than you ever gave yourself credit for.

PERSONAL PREFERENCES IN A SOCIAL CONTEXT

When you have completed your questionnaire, study the individual hobbies, leisure pursuits and the work you do in the community.

Ask yourself the following questions for each hobby etc and write down the answers.

1. Is the activity something you do on your own or in a group?
2. If it is a group activity, does it involve a single sex or a mixed sex group?
3. If it is a group activity, does it involve large numbers of people you might not know, or a small close-knit group of friends?
4. Is the activity indoor or outdoor?
5. Do you have to relate quickly to people you do not know?

Is there a regular pattern of preference or not? Do you always mix socially with a large number of other people? Are you happier on your own? Do you naturally gravitate towards certain groups? Are you the indoor or outdoor type? These are the sort of questions you can ask yourself.

From the answers you have given, do you think your

preferences can be transferred into a working environment? Conversely, are there some obvious work situations you would now want to avoid?

Making a choice

If you had to choose only *one* of your current spare time interests, which would it be? Think about this very carefully before you choose. Write down your decision and then state as fully as possible why you have made this choice.

Look at what your choice means in terms of the skills and abilities needed; the social context in which it takes place; and the personal motivation behind why you enjoy your involvement.

If you have chosen honestly, the item selected should provide you with one of the best indicators yet of the type of work you should be considering and the most appropriate working environment to suit you.

Reasons for doing what you do

Having looked at the social side of your spare time interests, turn next to *why* you do them.

Look through the questionnaire again. Select from the list below, the best description of the *motive* that lies behind your involvement. If you do something because you enjoy being a leader or because you are ambitious to achieve, don't be ashamed to admit it. This is your Self Portrait. It must reflect who you are. Write down the letters identifying your motives next to each interest and add up how many of each set of letters you have at the end. You may find you need to use more than one set to describe your reasons fully.

- self-expression   (SE)
- social contact   (SC)
- helping others   (HO)
- authority over others   (AO)
- personal challenge   (PC)

- prestige value   (PV)
- individual freedom   (IF)

Is there any one motive which is the clear leader, or is there a mix? Does this give you any clues about the sort of job and working environment you would feel comfortable in?

PERSONAL PREFERENCES IN THE CONTEXT OF YOUR JOB

Your motivational drives can be expressed in other terms – as qualities you display as part of your approach to your job. For example:

- Self-expression   =   creative
- Social contact   =   team orientated
- Helping others   =   caring
- Authority over others   =   able to lead
- Personal challenge   =   achievement orientated
- Prestige value   =   seeking a high profile
- Individual freedom   =   self-sufficient

Very often you see these qualities being asked for in job advertisements. For example – 'We are looking for someone who is able to work under pressure to a high standard as part of our dynamic sales force.' Roughly translated this means – 'We are looking for an achiever who can work as part of a team.'

Translate your own motivational drives into qualities which might be sought by an employer and write out a brief paragraph incorporating these in an advertisement for a fictitious vacant post.

CHECKLIST

- What hobbies and interests from your childhood have shaped your adult interests?

- Were these childhood interests self-generated, or through parental or other adult influences?

- Has personal initiative played a dominant role in your spare time pursuits?

- Have you learnt more about your range of skills and abilities by scrutinising your various interests?

- If so, have you identified any which you feel might become transferable skills in the job market?

- Does the total amount of time you spend on your hobbies etc each week almost match the amount of time you used to spend at work?

- Do you regard these outside activities as being less important/just as important/more important than work?

- Do you feel you have learnt anything about the sort of environment, level of activity and social mix that appeals to you most?

- If so, do you feel you could translate this into what you would like to see in a new career?

- Do you know what work situations you should avoid in future?

Before moving on to Chapter 5, record your progress against Milestones 18–25 in Appendix 1, pages 138–139.

5

How Do Others See Me?

STEPPING OUTSIDE YOURSELF

This chapter puts the finishing touches to your Self Portrait. Up to now you have been delving into your history, extracting your many and varied experiences, identifying your skills and abilities, and considering the motivational drives that make up who you are. You have been studying your special uniqueness.

Looked at as a whole, this exercise may have thrown up one or two surprising results: you may have cast a completely different light on events in your past, or your capabilities in the present; you may now feel some regret over certain actions, or satisfaction over the outcome of others. You may also have begun to feel more positive about making better use of the future.

The aim of this chapter is to stand back and study your finished picture. You should now feel confident you know yourself much better than you did before you began the exercise. But what about other people? They only see the finished 'portrait', not what went into its making. This can colour their attitude towards you and their perception of you as a person.

So what do they see? Does everyone 'see' the same person? Do you think you might make more of what you have to offer if you changed the 'image' in some way?

To answer these questions, you need to stand away from yourself and analyse how other people react to you in different situations, how this can affect your approach to them, and what you can learn from this interaction.

LIFE ROLES AND ROLE PLAY

It is true to say all of us show different images of ourselves to the outside world depending on the circumstances we face at the time. You can think of these various personae as a series of

masks, if you like. The 'real' us lying behind these masks may never be revealed to others, or may only be revealed at a time of crisis. This can present us with a problem: if we aren't careful, we can begin to live the life of the person *other people imagine we are*, because this is what they expect of us. This expectation can place a tremendous strain on the individual concerned, especially if he or she is effectively having to live a lie to match these expectations.

We all play a large number of roles in the course of our everyday life – rather like quick-change parts in a play – but we can only be successful in these roles if we feel comfortable in them. Playing a part we do not feel 'at home' in lowers our stress threshold and can make life unbearable after a while.

Roles within the family
Start at the beginning and think about the most obvious roles you have to play in life – those connected with your childhood place within a family, and the transition from childhood to adulthood with its changing demands. These are:

- child

- lover

- partner

- parent.

The child's role
In its simplified form, this is a role where you are subservient, totally dependent on others and need to be cared for and loved.

Your views are rarely if ever taken into consideration. You are expected to listen to older or more experienced people and be guided by them. You are not expected to take the initiative. You are instructed on what action to take and expected to carry this out. If you act your part well, you receive love and affection. If you do not, you run the risk of having these much-needed responses taken away. You are very vulnerable.

Some people carry this role into the adult world, usually with disastrous results.

The lover's role
The lover's role has a large element of the child in it: you are
dependent and need to be loved. The difference here is that your
part is not played for general consumption: it is aimed at one
person – the object of your desire who has some power over
you. But the subservience you display is no longer childlike: it
is no longer total. There is the expectation that at some stage the
other party will reciprocate, so that the power to hold in thrall
will pass back and forth, like a weight being passed between the
two sides of a pair of scales.

It is when this mutual passing back and forth stops that you
are left with an imbalance: one person has the ascendancy over
the other. The role and the mask that goes with it has changed:
you have become either the 'parent' or the 'child' on a
permanent basis and the relationship becomes unstable and
usually comes to an end.

The partner's role
The partner's role in generalised terms is one of mutual support.
You play a variety of parts to suit a variety of circumstances.
You can expect to play the lover, the child or the parent,
depending on the situation. Equally, you will expect your
partner to play the reciprocal role to maintain the balance of the
partnership. Equilibrium is maintained when both parties
understand their roles, and respond to situations by adopting the
right reciprocal role for the occasion. Disequilibrium sets in as
soon as one partner does not accept the role he or she is required
to play by the other and the element of partnership collapses.

The parental role
This role is a mixture of care, protection and dominance. You
are the initiator of actions, the leader, the decision-maker, the
controller of others. Subordination is all around you. You expect
to be listened to and your advice to be acted upon. You may
achieve your ends with a velvet glove or a mailed fist, but this
in no way affects the outcome. You may be extremely caring
and thoughtful of others, but you are nevertheless the one who is
very much in charge.

Some people take the autocratic side of the parental role out

of the family and into the wider world. This is the role that in the wrong hands and unmodified by other behavioural roles inevitably causes conflict when it comes up against other adult behavioural patterns.

Other roles in adult life

As adults, there are equivalent roles to those of child, partner and parent outside the family unit. These are seen in the way we respond to other people we meet or interact with during the course of our work or spare time interests.

Subordinate role
This is a childlike role in the adult world. You are told what to do and you get on with it.

This role is not restricted simply to the work environment: it can be seen in the way any two or more people respond to one another. Some will always be led by others, whether this is in a committee or a team activity. This does not necessarily mean, however, that they are happy about this state of affairs. They may very much wish to play a peer group role, or even take the initiative occasionally, but the presence of a more dominant member or members prevents this from happening.

Peer group role
This is the equivalent of the partnership role in the family. There is acceptance of others in a group as being equals, with reciprocal shifts of roles between members taking place to meet different situations. This is generally a very satisfying environment for all participants.

Dominant role
Here is the parental role, benevolent or otherwise, in operation in the adult world. It may not always be welcome or appropriate.

There is the obvious work equivalent in the 'boss', but there are others outside the workplace, such as committee chairman or team captain where, although leadership is required, it may well be counter-productive if it is autocratic in nature, or does not have the approval of the whole group.

Role play

Think about the whole range of roles you play in your
interaction with others during the course of an average day. You
will find you adopt and shift your role play in response to the
situation you are in, and to the mix of personalities around you.

One day in the life of . . .

At breakfast with your family you play two roles – that of
parent and partner – at the same time.

You take your child to school and have to ask the head
teacher for your child to have time off to go to the dentist. The
head teacher is a brusque and difficult person who clearly
regards you as an inferior. You would like to treat the matter on
a peer group basis but you are forced into a subordinate role.

You return home irritated by this encounter to find the
decorator who promised to come yesterday standing
apologetically on the doorstep trying to make excuses. You are
not pleased. You let him know this by your tone which places
you in the dominant role and pushes him very firmly into the
subordinate.

Later in the day a group of friends come round to discuss a
project you are all involved in. The discussion takes places at a
peer group level and everyone is amicable and at ease.

You collect your child from school and take over the parental
role again, adding the partnership role later over the tea table.

The phone rings. Your father would like to come and visit:
he hasn't been round for ages. Don't you care about him any
more? Will you come and collect him now? – he asks. You
respond in your child's role by complying with his wishes. He
joins the family circle, treating you as a child. This is an
uncomfortable situation: your partner is still operating at a
partnership level and your child wants you to provide a parental
role. You find it difficult or impossible to juggle all the roles
expected of you with the frequency required by this mixed
company. Your temper becomes frayed.

Supper time. You have taken your father home and discarded
the childhood role. You have tucked up your own child
and ceased to act the parent. Your partner has gone out to a
meeting.

At long last you are able to discard all your masks and allow yourself the luxury of being yourself.

Comment

You can see from this example that while you are happy in the role you are playing, or expected to play, there is no inner conflict. Conflict sets in the moment you are pushed into a role you do not feel is appropriate at the time. This is an important point to remember when you are looking for a new career. You must not try to persuade yourself into a situation which would be stressful to you.

EVALUATING YOUR ADULT ROLES OUTSIDE THE FAMILY

How do other people treat me?

Just as the roles we are expected to play within the family unit can produce stressful situations, so can those which are expected of us in the workplace and during our spare time activities. Studying these additional roles and their effect on us is the next task.

To do this, look at the *last* job you listed in the questionnaire 'Working History and Experience' on page 34 in Chapter 3, and *all* the activities you listed in the questionnaire 'Current Spare Time Interests' on page 54 of Chapter 4.

Consider both your job and spare time activities individually and think about what answers you would give to the following questions:

- Do people actively seek me out for advice or not?
- Do people listen to my opinion or ignore it?
- Do people act on my suggestions or not?
- Do people expect something from me or not?
- Do people give me responsibility or try to remove it?

Write down what you discover about the roles you played in the various situations you met in your workplace.

You are likely to find your answers will vary according to circumstances and the personalities of the people involved.

Looking at your last job for instance, you will in all probability discover a broad mix of roles was expected of you, depending on what duties you were carrying out at the time – such as supervising or being supervised, giving or taking instructions, or participating in a peer group exercise as part of a team of equals.

In your social life, you are likely to find an equally diverse role play dependent on the perception of you by others in your group – as well as their individual perceptions of themselves.

When you have finished look at your answers individually. Using any adjectives you feel are appropriate, how would you describe yourself from the point of view of each of the following:

- your boss

- your colleagues

- your subordinates

- your close friends

- your acquaintances.

Do they all see you in the same light, or do different facets of your personality come into play in different circumstances? Do you influence their vision of you by a conscious change of role to fit these circumstances? Do you now believe this is a good or a bad thing? Do you feel there are some situations where you would have preferred to adopt a different role? Why was this? What was it that stopped you from doing so?

Now consider the following:

- Do I try to appear approachable or not?
- Do I enjoy being sociable or not?
- Do I encourage others to give their opinion or not?
- Do I really want other people's opinion or not?
- Do I expect things from other people or not?
- Do I prefer to act on my own or with others?
- Do I give people responsibility or try to remove it?
- Am I prepared to act on other people's suggestions or not?
- Do I give the appearance of being a caring person or not?

From your answers, how much of your true self is visible to others? Are you projecting your true image or the 'mask' you think is acceptable to them in the role you are playing? Does this 'mask' make you feel better able to cope, or does it place a strain on you?

These questions are important because if you are starting out on a new career, you might well want to discard some of the 'masks' you have worn in certain situations in the past. You may want to adopt a softer profile, or a harder one. If so, recognise the fact you actively want to change other people's perceptions of you and ask yourself how you might be able to achieve this aim.

How do I react to other people's perception of me?

How you feel about the way other people treat you can give you some idea about whether or not the role you are playing at the time is one you feel 'at home' in in those particular circumstances.

Put yourself in all the various situations you meet on a day-to-day basis. Conjure up the emotions generated by the way other people respond to you both at work and in your spare time occupations. Are there specific circumstances where you feel:

- anger

- resentment

- acceptance

- contentment

- pleasure

- satisfaction

- indifference.

Is what you feel appropriate for the situation, or not? Are you feeling satisfied because you have put someone else down unnecessarily, or because you feel you have made a positive contribution to a situation? Is the anger you feel directed at someone else or at yourself? Is your acceptance of the way

others treat you due to your consenting to the status they have conferred on you, or a lack of confidence in your own abilities?

To put this into a nutshell, are you happy with the image you are projecting?

Are there any aspects I need to change?

When you are starting from scratch, you will almost certainly have to face a different set of roles from those you played in your last job.

Accepting guidance from others

In your new situation, you may need to retrain and accept guidance from others; you may have to listen before you can speak. In these circumstances you cannot afford to adopt the dominant role: it is misplaced and unacceptable. Instead, you must be prepared to adopt the lesser role of a willing subordinate until you have completed your training and become firmly established in your new career.

If you held a fairly senior position in your last job, perhaps where the majority of your duties and responsibilities meant you were taking the lead most of the time and directing others, you may find the mental readjustment necessary to meet your new circumstances quite daunting. Nonetheless, it is vital you recognise your changed circumstances and act accordingly. If you don't, your attitude will hinder your progress and prevent others from helping you to achieve your goal.

Bolstering your self-esteem

If you held a more humble position in your last job, however, you may have a different set of hurdles to cross. Your greatest problem may be buffing up your image rather than toning it down. Perhaps you need to improve your self-confidence or assertiveness. This is especially important if you want to 'sell' your skills and experience properly to a new employer, or financial backer, or to convince a college that you have the ability and vitality to be a successful mature student.

Your self-confidence is the first thing to suffer if you have had to cope with redundancy. Even after you have completed all the exercises in this book, and come to recognise you have

greater skills and abilities than you first imagined, you may still lack the confidence to sell yourself to the outside world.

If this is a major stumbling block for you, then do seriously consider joining a course at your local college or business centre to improve your assertiveness skills. Check with the course provider first to see which group of people the course is aiming to attract. Some may be designed to meet specific needs, such as those of women returners, or redundant managers, so make sure you choose a course which meets your own requirements. It is quite pointless putting yourself in a situation where your self-confidence could shrivel up completely because you were uncomfortable or felt out of place with the rest of the people in the group.

THE FINISHED PICTURE OF YOU

At this point, all the data gathering is complete – and so is your Self Portrait. Whether you like the picture you have painted of yourself or not, it should help you to focus more precisely on your strengths and concentrate on improving your weaknesses, if you have any.

Starting with the next chapter is the task of making sense of the data collected so far, using it as a guide to show you how to approach planning your future career path and the how to tackle the choices that have to be made.

CHECKLIST

- What role do you play most within the family unit? Would you prefer another role?

- What role do you or did you play most in the work environment? Would you prefer another role?

- What role do you play most in your spare time activities? Does it differ from your main family or work roles?

- What have you discovered about your projected image?

- Is your projected image what you intend it to be in every circumstance? If not, why not?

- Are you projecting an image which does not reflect your personality? If so, does this help you cope with particular circumstances or produce stress?

- Are there any images you want to discard in your new career? If so, what are they and why do you want to discard them?

- Are there any images you want to foster in your new career? If so, how do you think you might be able to do this?

- How do you believe starting a new career will affect both your self-image and the image you want to project?

- Are you anxious about adapting to new roles? If so, how do you think you might be able to overcome this?

Before moving on to Chapter 6, record your progress against Milestones 26–30 in Appendix 1, page 139.

6

Making Sense of the Data

PULLING THE STRANDS TOGETHER

The aim of this chapter is to help you with your revision, rather along the same lines as if you were about to take an examination. You have completed the coursework, now you need to brush up on the important points you have identified and bring these together into a meaningful whole.

At this stage, it is probably worth repeating what was said at the start of Chapter 1 – that to succeed in a new career you have to target your new job very precisely; you must be confident you know where you are going, and why; and that the clues to help you achieve this confidence lie in your own personal history.

Now you have a detailed study of your personal history to hand in the form of your Self Portrait, the next step is to re-read everything. There are two very good reasons for doing this. They are:

1. You need to refresh your memory, particularly if you completed the exercises in Chapters 2 – 5 over a longish period; and
2. You need to give extra thought to the points you took the trouble to identify as being especially important as you worked your way through the questionnaires, and why you felt these were significant enough to commit to paper.

There is always the temptation to rush through this procedure – DON'T. Make this a leisurely progress. Absorb everything, consider everything, particularly if you find you have written a comment which on reflection no longer seems to have much relevance, or is certainly less important to you at this stage than it was earlier. You felt it was important at the time so don't ignore it, or even worse, discard it. Try to remember what it was

that made you feel you should draw attention to this point at the time: it could be very relevant.

And most important of all – try not to let your previous *type* of career, or careers, blinker your thinking. You want to free yourself from all previously conceived notions about what is right for you and start from the beginning with a clean sheet.

PERSONAL NEEDS AND SATISFACTION

A really successful career should meet your needs as an individual and give you the maximum of satisfaction in the process. To do this, it has to:

- take place in the right environment;
- reflect your true personality;
- make the optimum use of your skills and abilities; and
- reflect as far as possible your main motivational drives.

Anything less than this is unlikely to be the right sort of job for you.

What is the right working environment for me?

The most obvious clue to this question lies in the answers you gave in setting out the pros and cons of each job you did in the past (Chapter 3), and in particular which of all your previous jobs you were prepared to say you enjoyed the most.

Was this:

- a solitary job, or were you part of a team?
- employment in a small, medium or large scale organisation?
- a job with the minimum supervision, or were you closely monitored?
- an indoor or outdoor job?
- physically or mentally demanding?
- office based or mobile?

- involving moves from location to location as part of your career progression?

- with plenty of opportunities for training and promotion?

- with colleagues younger, older or the same age range?

- with colleagues the same sex as you and did this matter to you?

From your answers, you should begin to see the type of working environment you prefer and which is likely to give you the most satisfaction. If you thoroughly enjoyed working as a member of a team in a large organisation where a large proportion of your working day was mobile, be aware of this working environment preference. Keep it firmly in mind. Don't let yourself forget it.

What if I didn't like any of my previous work environments?
It is possible if you were going down the wrong road in your career that every job you did, or your entire working life ran counter to your inner self. You will know this if you had difficulty in actually choosing which of your jobs you enjoyed most. In your heart of hearts you knew you didn't like any of them.

If this is the case then look at the choice you made under the heading 'What would I like to do in future?' on page 39 in Chapter 3. Look again at what you have written in terms of the work environment you thought you might prefer. Does this still hold true now at the end of the exercise, or have you modified your ideas in any way?

If your ideas are still unfocused at this stage, don't let this bog you down. Turn to the answers you gave to 'Personal preferences in a social context' on page 55 in Chapter 4. What do these tell you?

- Did you find a social pattern emerging in your choice of hobbies?

- What sort of environment would this constitute if transferred to the workplace?

- Would you be working with people of your own age?

- Would you be working on your own or in a group?

And so on. If you still can't see your way clearly, leave the problem for a while and come back to it later. Often allowing yourself breathing space helps the thought processes.

THE PERSONALITY FACTOR

What is my true personality?
In Chapter 5 we saw how it is possible to present a whole series of different 'selves' to the outside world while our 'real self' remains hidden away. We also saw the problems that can spring from trying to act out a role which others impose on us when this runs counter to our natural inclinations.

For clues as to your true personality, ignore your work history. Concentrate instead on all the information you gathered together in response to Chapter 4. Your spare time interests are far better indicators. Remember, these are what you do because you *want* to, not because you *have* to.

Under the heading 'Reasons for doing what you do' on page 56, you should have identified the motives behind your involvement in each of your pastimes under the following headings:

- self-expression

- social contact

- helping others

- authority over others

- personal challenge

- prestige value

- individual freedom.

If one motive stood out clearly above the rest, have you recognised that this constitutes an important facet of your personality? It will therefore need to have a high profile in

whatever career you decide upon.

If no clear leader emerged from your list, pay attention to those motives which still rank higher than the others. Which are they? Identify them because they each represent an important part of your personality which needs to be catered for.

What else can I discover about myself?

Look again at your pastimes.

* Do group activities have a large part to play?

* Do you hold any leadership roles, such as team captain or chairman? Are there any creative or scientific interests?

* Are all your pastimes solitary?

* Is there an element of risk involved – in the widest sense?

In a nutshell, what do your hobbies say about you?

Do they tell you that you are solitary or gregarious, reserved or outwardly expressive, a thinker or a doer, a leader or a follower? Do you feel this is probably a true picture of your real self? If not, why not? Remember the influence of other people discussed in Chapter 5. If you feel frustrated by the domineering personality of others in any of your pastimes, then recognise part of your personality includes a degree of lack of self-confidence, or insecurity. Don't feel overwhelmed by this knowledge: it is not an insurmountable problem and may be due entirely to very specific circumstances which would not apply in other areas of your life. It is certainly something which with the right sort of guidance can be modified or even overcome.

Look at what you have discovered about yourself and put this into a work context. If you enjoy solitary hobbies, you are hardly likely to feel at ease working as part of a team, just as if you prefer group activities, a job where you are working in isolation would be totally inappropriate. Equally frustrating would be a situation where your creative or analytical mind was thwarted by repetitive routines or haphazard working practices.

SKILLS AND ABILITIES

How can I make the best use of them?

First of all, you have to recognise what your skills and abilities are.

There are the more obvious ones which can be picked out from your educational attainments, such as literacy, numeracy or language skills. There are the additional ones which come with attaining professional or academic qualifications as well as those acquired through on-the-job training or experience. These skills can range from complex processes such as those essential to a brain surgeon, to the everyday variety such as being able to answer the telephone and communicate satisfactorily with other people.

Don't forget or undervalue the skills which do not belong to the workplace. In Chapter 4 when you were completing the questionnaire on your pastimes, you were asked to list the skills or specialist knowledge you needed in each of your hobbies or community roles. Remind yourself of these now.

Go back to Chapter 2 and your formative years. Did you develop any skills within the family which are still relevant but which you tend to take largely for granted – such as, caring for an elderly relative or handicapped sibling, coping with personal tragedy or taking responsibility at an early age?

Don't discount anything which can still be put to use, even if you really don't want to use the skill or knowledge on a day-to-day basis: it may be a useful secondary skill which is essential to achieving your main aim. You may hate driving, but if your new career is entirely dependent on your ability to be mobile, then it would obviously be foolish not to recognise the importance of being able to drive. You should be aiming to find a career which will use your best skills to their best advantage while allowing many of your lesser abilities the chance to play their part.

MATCHING CAREER TO MOTIVATIONAL DRIVES

In what way should my new career reflect these?

Go back to Chapter 4 and the 'Reasons for doing what you do' on page 56. Study the main motives you identified which lay

behind your commitment to these pastimes. Your new career *must* satisfy the emotional needs these drives represent or you will never be able to put your heart and soul into the venture.

Don't delude yourself into thinking you can ignore them, especially if that is precisely what you have done in the past. If your desire for self-expression is high, then persuading yourself it is socially more acceptable or responsible to devote yourself to caring for others does nothing either for you or the people you are supposed to be helping. You have to be totally honest with yourself. Anything less will distort the picture and give you false guidelines.

In studying the motivational drives that affect your choice of pastime, you may have noticed one rather obvious omission in the list. This omission rarely applies to hobbies – unless you have included 'Investing on the Stock Market' as one of your paramount pastimes – but almost always applies to the world of work. This is:

- making money.

This drive does not necessarily play a major role, but if you need to work in order to keep both yourself and your dependants above the poverty line, it has a relevance you quite literally can't afford to ignore.

What importance do you place on making money?

- Has this motivational drive played a large part in your working life up until now?

- Do you still feel you want it to?

- Do you need the satisfaction of a high monetary return for what you do?

Don't shunt this motivation into a siding. Face it and answer it honestly.

COMPARING CAREER HISTORY WITH HOBBIES

Looking for compatibility

Ideally, your working life should satisfy your needs and expectations in the same way as your pastimes do. Put in its simplest form, if there is a good match, you are likely not only to succeed, but to flourish. If there is a poor match, or even a complete mis-match, success will be achieved only at great personal cost, often resulting in the onset of stress related illnesses.

The greatest problem with a mis-match is that you can give the impression of being very successful at your job – even to yourself. You perform well because you are determined to succeed at all costs. Any inner doubts or misgivings are suppressed by your drive to take on a challenge. This situation isn't helped because you will also have the right skills to achieve this illusory success. There's nothing wrong with the skills, it's the working environment that needs changing.

Look for compatibility under the following headings:

- skills and abilities

- level of responsibility

- environment

- social mix.

Skills and abilities

Does your career history or your last full-time permanent job reflect the range of skills and abilities you know you have? Does it utilise some but not others? Which skills are under-utilised or not used at all? Are these skills 'high profile' in your non-working environment? Take note of this if they are.

Level of responsibility

Compared with your spare time occupations, how does your last work role rate? Did it involve a similar range of responsibilities, fewer or greater? If there is an obvious disparity, do you feel this is something you need to bear in mind?

Environment

Do your leisure activities take place in the same sort of environment as your work, such as in an artistic or scientific, technical or theoretical context; in large or small groups, or on your own? If the two environments do not match up, did you consciously choose these leisure activities as a positive reaction against your working environment? If this is the case, don't ignore such an obvious move on your part to give your personal needs a much needed outlet to express themselves.

Social mix

Do the people you choose to mix with in your spare time mirror the age range and sex of your immediate working group? If they do not, is this a conscious move on your part? Have you any hang-ups about working with certain groups of people? If you have, now is the time to own up and admit it to yourself.

RECONCILING THE FACTS

Building on what you know

At this point go back to Chapter 3 once again and what you wrote under the heading 'What would I like to do in the future?' on page 39.

This exercise was designed to be a taster, to get you thinking not only about what you might like to do in the future, but also in what context.

Look through what you wrote down then in the light of what you now know about your preferred work environment, your personality, your skills and abilities, and of course, your motivational drives. Was the result of your brainstorming closer to the mark than you expected? If so, you have a strong basis for being more confident about planning your future. If not, don't give up. All is not lost.

The perfect job

Using all the information you now have about your personal preferences, your skills and abilities, write out a job description which in your opinion would meet all your personal needs and aspirations. Make this as broad as possible

for maximum benefit. Don't forget to include the qualities you identified in Chapter 4 on pages 56 and 57. Also include the level of financial returns if this is an important factor to be considered.

The job to be avoided
This exercise is the exact opposite of the previous one to help you identify everything you would not want to see in a job. When completing this, you must feel very strongly about what you see as the most undesirable elements. Use as a guideline the fact you would *never* consider taking a job or embarking on a career which had any of these facets. They must not be mild irritants which could possibly be overcome by some means or other.

The overall picture

What you have uncovered about yourself during this voyage of discovery might not be what you wanted to see. You may have even come to realise you are an entirely different person from the image you present to the outside world. You may have acted out this role for years and convinced yourself the mask you wore was the 'real' you.

You may have identified times in your life when you made the wrong choices, or had these forced on you by circumstances beyond your control. You may have made career decisions on a totally wrong premise. And you may well have discovered you did not understand yourself well enough to take control of the situation sooner.

On the other hand, you may have come up with answers that seem to point in exactly the same direction as you were going before; where your life seems to have been well-planned from every point of view and your basic needs and aspirations have been largely catered for. In this case it is the small differences that have become important in your life, whether these are in the context of the work environment, the job content, or the level of responsibility. Considering what to do under these circumstances will be discussed in Chapter 7. Facing the need to break new ground will be dealt with in Chapter 8.

CHECKLIST

- What have you identified as being the right working environment for you?

- What are the personal needs and aspirations you have identified which make up your personality?

- What are your skills and abilities? Which of these do you consider to be the most important?

- What are your motivational drives? Is there any one drive which is the clear leader and which is it?

- Do the skills and abilities you use in your pastimes match those which you use in the workplace? If not, why not?

- Do the roles you take on out of the workplace reflect your status within the workplace? If not, why not?

- Do your leisure activities take place in a similar environment to your work activities? If not, why not?

- Do you concentrate your leisure activities with the same age and sex as those of your immediate working group? If not, why not?

- What do you see as being your perfect job?

- What aspects of a job or career would you find impossible to accept?

Before moving on to Chapter 7, record your progress against Milestones 31–37 in Appendix 1, pages 139–140.

7

Rethinking Your Old Career

COMING TO TERMS WITH A U-TURN

It is easy to become disheartened when situations work out differently from the way you anticipated. This is especially true if at the beginning of this book you were convinced you needed to break away from your old career, but gradually realised, as you worked your way through the process of getting to know yourself better, that you had no sound reason for making such a dramatic change. Try not to be too disappointed. In Chapter 1 it was emphasised that starting a new career was far from being an easy option. It represents a great deal of commitment and hard work and should never be underestimated.

What you are facing now is a new type of challenge – putting your old career into a new and hopefully better perspective by extracting the best parts of it and giving these a greater say in what you intend to do in the future.

IMPROVING YOUR CHANCES IN THE SAME CAREER

Your attitude to the job search

Before sitting down and scouring the situations vacant columns, remind yourself of what you want to achieve. You wanted to change your career. Now you have discovered you do not need to discard your past experience in its entirety. Instead, you need to reshape it. This is an important point, because the last thing you should do now is plunge yourself despairingly into the exact replica of your previous job. Remember, something was wrong with that job as far as you were concerned, and the exercises you worked through to build up your Self Portrait should have helped you to identify precisely what this was.

Restate your reasons for wanting to start again

Start by refreshing your memory as to the reason why you wanted to make a career change in the first place – or thought this would provide the answer to all your woes. Under the heading 'Why do I want to change my career?' on page 8 of Chapter 1, you wrote down a simple statement giving your reasons for this decision. Is this statement still valid? Have you identified any other factors since which should have been included, or which should replace the original statement now that you have had time to reflect more fully on all the circumstances? Rewrite your statement if you now feel your reasons need to be redefined.

PERSONAL FACTORS TO CONSIDER

Level of responsibility

The strict hierarchy of UK organisations has undergone dramatic change in the recent past. Large numbers of middle management positions have disappeared and employees are expected to expand their roles to meet the 'multi-tasking' ethos of today. Promotion therefore may be reflected in financial reward for meeting targets or standards rather than upward movement within the organisational structure.

Greater or lesser responsibilty
Frustration generated by being held back, or by not being given the opportunity to shine, can demoralise the best motivated of individuals. But beware of overestimating your potential.

- Did you fail to progress because your employer had no properly structured training or promotion policy?

- Were you blocked by personal animosity or indifference by your superiors?

- Do you believe your abilities were undervalued or unrecognised?

- Had you got as far up the ladder as your abilities allowed you to go?

- Would your frustration have evaporated if you had been offered opportunities to broaden your experience or skills within the existing organisational structure?

In all these discussions with yourself, it is crucial you recognise the upper limit of your own potential. If you do not, you can become an excellent example of *The Peter Principle*, where you are promoted or seek promotion beyond the point where you can work to the best of your ability.

An over-promoted individual is as unhappy as his or her underpromoted counterpart. In this case, the unhappiness stems from the struggle to maintain a satisfactory job performance in the face of potential failure.

Existing commitments

Will your personal commitments or those of your dependants have any bearing on your job search? A quick run through Chapter 2 should remind you of this if you have forgotten. Once again, remember not to underestimate these commitments, whether they are domestic, social or financial: they can affect the location and type of job you are looking for, as well as the level of responsibility that goes with it.

When you study the situations vacant pages, keep your commitments to the forefront of your mind and don't get carried away by your own misplaced enthusiasm for a job. Job advertisements can be minefields of hidden meanings. Consider the following:

> Looking for a change of environment? Here is a challenging opportunity for a self-motivated person with a positive go-getting approach. You will be expected to maintain high standards of output in a busy work situation. Extra hours will be needed at short notice during the summer months. An excellent rewards package is available for the right person.

Who is the 'right person' this organisation looking for?

- someone with plenty of vitality who is able to work under pressure
- someone who can work unsupervised

- someone who is prepared to put in extra hours at the drop of a hat.

In other words, someone who is prepared to put their job before anything else.

Recognising yourself
You might indeed be looking for a change of environment. Also, if you are out of a job for any length of time, you can often be pressurised into seeking a 'challenging' role, into being 'self-motivated' and having a 'positive approach'. In fact, this is the standard knee-jerk response frequently expected of you by the Pick-yourself-up-and-get-on-with-Life Brigade. But can you put in the extra hours that would be required, and what level of pressure would you be working under?

What you have to be aware of is your present circumstances are unlikely to match those which existed at the time you took up your last job. This is even more the case if you worked your way up the promotional ladder within the same organisation, and did not have to face the employment market for several years. Your perception of yourself may be several years out of date and if you are not careful, you can become the equivalent of the ageing actor or actress auditioning for one of the leading roles in *Romeo and Juliet.*

Stereotypical age groups
The Chartered Institute of Personnel and Development (CIPD) has been critical of the use of age limits in job vacancy advertisements for many years. A European Directive will bring ageism into line with other forms of unlawful discrimination in employment, but legislation in the UK will not take effect until 2006 at the earliest. In the meantime a voluntary code of practice *Age Diversity in Employment* has been introduced urging employers to make use of the huge resource pool of older workers who are increasingly becoming a sizeable proportion of the workforce. In many cases there is no justifiable reason for these age restrictions – anyone of any age with the proper qualifications could easily do the job in question. In other cases, however, employers are seeking the

commitment level they associate with the stereotyped image of a particular age group. This stereotyping exists even when no age is actually specified in the advert, as in the example above, but it is clear from the wording used that a particular type of candidate is expected to apply.

When you apply for jobs, you need to be aware of the existence of this stereotyping and appreciate its implications. Set out below is a very rough guide to what might be expected. There are both good and bad points from the employer's point of view.

1. **If you are less than 29 years of age,** you are likely to be
    single or newly married
    ambitious to succeed
    fully mobile
    energetic and innovative
    easier to train
    more prepared to take risks
    prepared to change employers more frequently
    eager for increased status and financial reward.

2. **If you are 30-39 years of age,** you are likely to be
    married with a family
    moderately ambitious
    less mobile because of family commitments
    less energetic or innovative
    slower to train
    more concerned with financial security than taking risks
    have a greater loyalty to the organisation.

3. **If you are 40 years of age or over,** you are likely to be
    not nearly as ambitious as you were
    possibly planning for early retirement
    much less energetic or innovative
    difficult to retrain
    resistant to organisational change
    unwilling to move location
    committed to the organisation
    unlikely to be looking for another employer.

This stereotyping is quite plainly an over-simplification. It would be difficult to describe either Winston Churchill or Barbara Cartland as being 'over the hill' after they reached the age of forty. There are always exceptions. But for many of us there is a grain of truth lying behind these broad assumptions. We are not what we were ten or twenty years ago, and our needs shift and adapt to our changing circumstances.

If you want to apply for a job which is clearly labelled, or one which implies it is being aimed at applicants outside your own age band, you need to do two things.

1.   Make sure you understand the assumptions which lie behind the stereotyped image of the perfect candidate and be certain you can meet the demands that will be expected of you without causing a personal crisis of some sort; and

2.   Aim to overcome the in-built prejudice of stereotyping by stressing your ability to meet the challenges of the 'hidden' requirements of the job.

Financial requirements

Can you afford to do what you want to do? This is a topic which will be looked at in greater depth in Chapter 9. For now, bear in mind that no matter how determined you are to start again, you may have to modify your plans in some way to satisfy your financial needs.

OTHER FACTORS TO TAKE INTO ACCOUNT

These can include:

* change of organisation

* change of status

* change of working environment

- change of living/working location
- change of skills base.

Change of organisation
You should now know from what you have discovered about
your personal preferences whether you would be happier
working in a small, medium or large scale organisation. If you
have been a solicitor in a large practice with specialities divided
between the partners, you may prefer the smaller concern where
each partner carries out a wider variety of services. If you have
been working in a small engineering enterprise, you may be
looking for a larger, more influential company.

Change of status
Changing your status involves a conscious decision to move up
or down the ladder to meet your personal needs. It is basically
about being more ambitious, or less, or ambitious in a different
direction – to achieve in other areas.

This is quite distinct from a change in the level of
responsibility. You can be the supervisor in charge of three or
fifty employees, or a district manager in charge of three or
twenty locations, but you are still a supervisor or a district
manager – there is just more, or less, responsibility. Titles can
often be extremely flexible in what they mean. This is very
helpful in situations where you might feel some anxiety about
appearing to lose face if you know you are taking a job which
has an obvious drop in status.

Change of working environment
Again this should reflect your personal preferences. You can be
a sales rep travelling the length and breadth of the country if
meeting people is your forte and you enjoy being on the road.
But you can equally well be a good salesman or woman by
using telemarketing techniques if your persuasive manner is at
its best over the phone and you prefer to be office based.
Choose the environment that suits you best.

Case study: Fighting frustration in the wrong environment

Alicia Sharp was 25. She was an only child of ambitious middle-class academic parents, sailed through school and achieved a good Honours degree in French. Her self-image was of a highly capable person who would automatically make it to the top.

Alicia joined a large retail chain as a management trainee and within three years was training graduate entrants herself. Although this was a responsible role, she realised she had been sidetracked in her ambition. Resentment set in and she set about looking for new jobs in a marketing role with large blue chip organisations. However, her applications were consistently turned down.

Alicia's problem lay in her perception of herself and the openings she had imagined would be hers by virtue of a degree. She was in fact quite average in her abilities, not particularly numerate and would have found working under pressure on financial analysis and organisational problem solving a great strain. The blue chip organisations had identified these weaknesses in their recruitment tests. Her strong points lay in her personality, her need to impress, influence and perform. Although her training post had provided her with an outlet for her talents, it had been in a completely wrong culture. She needed a status title, a colourful environment and a team of colleagues with similar personalities.

Alicia was helped to identify the right environment for her and pointed in the direction of public relations. She very swiftly became promotions and PR manager for a group of commercial radio stations.

Change of living/working location

This change could be forced on you if you are in a locality bristling with hundreds of other job seekers with precisely the same skills as yourself and a dwindling market for them. This is presuming, of course, that a market still exists for your skills in other parts of the UK. If it does not, then you are faced with the

need to update your skills base to find similar employment (see below).

Relocation is a difficult option. If you are considering it, and have a family to think of, look back at all the issues raised in Chapter 2 under the heading 'Your Family Now' on page 28. If you dealt with these some time ago, make sure that none of the circumstances have changed over the passage of time and that your data is still correct. If the situation has changed and raised new issues which need to be resolved, they must be sorted out *at the earliest possible opportunity* so that everyone likely to be directly affected by a move has the chance to express their hopes or fears and feels able to support you. You must be prepared for the possibility that they may not, or that your decision has come at a crucial time in someone else's life. Resolution of these difficulties will have to come from within the family unit if you are not to create more problems than you overcome.

Change of skills base

You may say you can't teach an old dog new tricks, but if you possess skills and experience which have become outdated, you must accept the fact that unless you are willing to retrain, the chances of finding another job will become very slim indeed.

The learning curve, as it is known, may flatten out as we get older, but this does not mean that we cease to be able to learn – it might just take a little longer. If you can build on what you already know and take on the challenge of new technology – which is one of the key factors in the new industrial and commercial revolution – then you become far more employable. You are also showing a level of determination and commitment which will act in your favour with a potential future employer.

Help with the latest local and national initiatives set up to retrain people who need to update their skills to match current requirements of industry, business and commerce can be obtained through your Local Skills Council in England, the Education and Training Department of the Scottish Executive, and others, such as Business Link and Jobcentres. Make use of the many and varied options open to you to enhance your chances in the employment market.

SHIFTING THE EMPHASIS

This is all about making use of your skills and experience in a slightly different way than you were using them before. It can be thought of as a half-way house between sticking with your old career and starting off on a completely new tack.

Case study: Accentuating the positive

Richard Batchelor was 31. He had an undistinguished education at a good public school, failing his A-levels. Both his teachers and his family considered him to have a low capability. As a result, he was pushed into studying for a Diploma in Agriculture and Business, which nonetheless helped him secure a good job as a Farm Manager handling the large estates of a Duke. Richard however, had no interest in practical agriculture. What he was really interested in – and was good at – was running the business side of the job.

With the downturn in the fortunes of agriculture, the Duke decided to give up his farming operations and Richard was faced not only with redundancy but also the loss of his home.

Richard's main motivational drives were directed towards business and commerce: motivating staff, increasing production, negotiating costs and sales, combined with excellent technical management ability which, much to his amazement, was discovered to be of post-graduate level. He wanted to achieve, enjoyed the challenges of change, was innovative, and was a leader rather than a follower.

Richard was encouraged to see that his skills, competencies and qualities could be transferred to other commercial environments, initially within the world of agriculture. He was persuaded to pursue this course of action while considering taking an MBA Degree to confirm the evidence of his abilities.

Within six months of seeking professional vocational guidance, Richard had obtained the newly created post of Commercial Development Executive with a large European agricultural chemical organisation.

In other words, don't discard your previous experience entirely: use it in a different way, expand on it. This way you are not only carving out a better future for yourself, you have the additional

satisfaction of knowing you are making the best use of the knowledge you have acquired in the past.

CHECKLIST

- What level of responsibility will you be looking for in your next job?

- What domestic, social and financial commitments do you have which might affect your job search?

- Can you identify what aspects of stereotyping will help/hinder you in your job search?

- How do you intend to overcome those which might hinder you?

- What size of organisation do you want to work for in the future?

- Do you intend to change your status with your next job? If so, in what direction and why?

- What type of working environment will you be looking for in your next job?

- Will you need to relocate? If so, what problems do you face and how do you intend to overcome these?

- Do you need to update your skills base? If so, what action do you intend to take to do so?

- Do you see ways in which you might transfer your existing skills and experience to other uses? If so, what openings do you think you could pursue?

Before moving on to Chapter 8, record your progress against Milestones 38–47 in Appendix 1, pages 140–141.

8

Breaking New Ground

FACING THE CHALLENGE

Discovering there has been a mis-match between your
motivational drives and your previous career is likely to produce
one of two effects.

1. Relief that at last you have been able to put your finger on
    why you have been frustrated or bored in your last job, or
    unsettled at the prospect of looking for a similar type of job
    again; or

2. Depressed that so many years of your life have been spent
    apparently going in the wrong direction to no good effect.

Depression is understandable, particularly if you have been
struggling against your inner self to succeed against all the odds.
But don't allow this negative thinking to persist. Experience is
rarely wasted, even if it has been a bad experience.
Understanding why it has been a bad experience is the clue to
your future success.

Case study: Giving in without a fight

Thirty-two-year-old John Bailey's passion was science. His
choices at A-level were a foregone conclusion, although his
decision to become a vegetarian made him drop Biology for
Geography. He had a very strong desire to help the environment
and wanted to become an ecologist. His confidence in his
mission however, was badly dented by only just scraping
through his degree in Environmental Science.

Believing he was not good enough to pursue his original
goal, he made no attempt to apply for scientific work and joined
the ranks of the graduate unemployed, drifting into jobs for the

money rather than any personal satisfaction. Seven years after graduating, he found himself as a high pressure salesman where he was not only out of his depth but working completely against his character. He felt he had wasted his life and saw nowhere to go.

John sought help from a vocational guidance adviser and discovered all his scientific, creative and practical interests were still very much alive and kicking. He was identified as a truly gifted person. Added to this, he was shown that his personality was that of a quiet introvert and thinker, in complete contrast to what he had been trying to be as a pushy salesman.

John was encouraged to see that his early choices at school had been correct; that his natural motivation, ability and disposition to be an ecologist had been right all along. The problem stemmed from the fact he had not been advised at the time that a mediocre degree did not prevent him from pursuing this goal.

Armed with a reference based on his guidance assessment, John gained a postgraduate place at University to study Environmental Impact Assessment and was offered two jobs before completing his final exams, the second as a scientist for an environmental consultancy which not only matched his exact requirements, but had the added bonus of being very well paid.

RECOGNISING YOUR GOAL

At the end of Chapter 6, were you able to flesh out your original career ideas you brainstormed in Chapter 3? Do you now know precisely:

- What you want to do?

- What level you would want to work at, or aim to work at?

- What sort of working environment you would be in?

- What additional facets you would want to see in the job?

The chances are that your head is full of good ideas, but these are still largely unformed, either because you do not have

sufficient information to hand on the career in question, or because you have insufficient knowledge of what possible careers might be open to you. Without this additional knowledge, you will not be able to answer the following questions:

- What retraining might be necessary?

- How long will this take?

- How will this be financed?

- What opportunities exist in this field?

- Is it likely I will have to move somewhere else to find employment?

- What are the financial rewards?

FINDING THE ANSWERS

Personal contacts

These can be your most valuable source of information. If you know anyone who is already working in the type of job you are thinking of, ask them to spare you some time to take you through all the aspects of the work involved. Press them on the pros and cons so you are certain about what you are going to be taking on.

Works of reference

Without personal contacts, you will need to turn to other sources of information.

Your local library, Jobcentre or Careers Service Office can help you here with reference books which you can study at your leisure. The address of your nearest Jobcentre appears under Jobcentre Plus in *The Phone Book*.

Occupations published by HMSO is available at Jobcentres and libraries. This covers around 600 jobs and careers of all types from the unskilled to professional. There are details on pay, opportunities, prospects, personal characteristics needed, entry requirements, training, whether you can be a late entrant

or not, and gives details of related occupations, eg actor – speech therapist, and sections on further information and reading.

There are many books available in libraries offering help and advice on a range of possible options, such as:

- volunteering

- opportunities abroad

- retraining

- becoming a mature student

- considering self-employment.

Some books are also available in CD-ROM format at a price. *Opportunities* has hypertext links enabling access to websites of professional bodies and organisations.

Professional bodies

If you are aiming for a profession, you should contact the recognised professional regulating body for any relevant information. This is particularly important where examination or experience qualifications will be expected of you before you can be admitted to the profession, or where you will not be allowed to practise without being a paid-up member of the professional body. Most professional bodies now have websites where you can access this information.

Some professional organisations provide advice and guidance to their members. The Institute of Financial Services for example, provides its members with career management and career counselling services to support those wanting to take control of their career progression.

Training providers

For non-professional training outlets, the *Yellow Pages* phone book for your area will give you a whole range of possibilities under the heading 'Training Services'. However, it is not always clear from individual entries precisely what training is on offer or who it is aimed at. You could waste a great deal of time and money in working your way methodically through the list. There

is also the danger that you do not have any way of measuring the quality of the training on offer.

Your best bet is to contact your local Jobcentre or Learning and Skills Council in the first instance. You will be able to discuss your training needs with them and they will be able to direct you to the most appropriate training provider to suit your requirements. There is also a wide range of adult learning contact addresses and government learning initiatives listed on the Education section of the Directgov website www.direct.gov.uk.

Learning and Skills Councils
Learning and Skills Councils are locally based throughout England and are responsible for post-16 and adult learning. Details of your nearest LSC are in *The Phone Book* or you can access information through the national website www. lsc.gov.uk. In Scotland, there is useful information on the websites www.careers-scotland.org.uk and www.scotland.gov.uk

Local colleges
Contacting your local college for their latest prospectus is the easiest way of finding out what is available locally.

Distance learning
If you can't find what you want locally and know immediately your commitments will prevent you from studying away from home, the wide variety of distance learning packages now available mean you can study practically anything by fitting your study sessions into available free hours.

The Open University is the most obvious immediate choice for degree courses but there are also personal interest home study packs available. Information on courses can be obtained from:

The Open University
Walton Hall
Milton Keynes
MK7 6AA
Tel: (01908) 274066
Fax: (01908) 653744

The OU website www.open.ac.uk not only provides details of all the courses on offer, but other useful guidance on careers although many of the extremely useful topics covered are only available if you are registered with the university.

Many professional bodies have distance learning programmes for their students which you could enquire about. Correspondence colleges were the original providers of distance learning for several professional bodies and many are still providing excellent opportunities for home-based students. A list of accredited colleges and the courses they offer is available from:

The Open and Distance Learning Quality Council
16 Park Crescent
London W1B 1AH
Tel: (020) 7612 7090
Fax: (020) 7612 7092
Email: info@odlqc.org.uk
Website: http://www.odlqc.org.uk

Although the Council is an independent body, it was set up at the request of government in 1969 to help raise standards in open and distance education and training to protect the interest of students. Accreditation includes rigorous assessment of a college's administrative and tutorial methods, educational materials and publicity. Accredited colleges are monitored and reassessed at regular intervals.

NOT RECOGNISING YOUR GOAL

This is not an improbable situation. If you have never had any idea from an early age as to the direction you wanted to take, the mass of data you have acquired in building up your Self Portrait will have given you very detailed information about the sort of person you are, the type of working environment which would suit you best, what your skills and experience are – but no focal point in which to direct them.

If it is any comfort, there are a lot of people in the same position.

Case study: Going nowhere fast

While at comprehensive school, Lynn Florence's only notion was to go to art school and become a 'colourful person'. She graduated with a degree in Fine Art and then discovered how uncolourful the reality of making a living could be. Unable to come to any definite decision, she went to Italy, taught English as a foreign language, married an Italian and lived very colourfully for eight years until her marriage broke up.

Returning to England, Lynn was alone, aged 38, without contacts and needing to support herself. She saw her only options as teaching Art or doing secretarial work. She was only able to secure part-time or temporary teaching jobs, so she completed a secretarial course to bridge the gap. For the following seven years her chequered history, with no evidence of commitment, ensured she never secured a full-time job. Her 'home' life was equally unstable: she lived in a mobile home, unable to break out of the vicious circle of low pay and insecurity to take control of her life and improve her prospects. She was very depressed and approaching a mid-life crisis.

Seeking vocational guidance, she was shown that although she had strong artistic interests, her strength lay in her very high verbal ability. Her motivational drives reflected her early aesthetic ambitions, but also highlighted the fact that she needed a more academic analytical challenge combined with a need to help people. She had a strong caring streak, inventiveness, independence and a great deal of commitment and drive which would never have been imagined from her work history.

Lynn had started her working life with low expectations and a fear of failure and had created her own cul-de-sac by avoiding challenges. She had never used her real abilities and values. By mid-life, she felt lost and without any sense of purpose.

Lynn was shown that her artistic and sensitive traits needed to be deployed in a professional role where she could be creative and progressive; that she was a facilitator who should be in a caring role, and most important of all, that her investment in art and teaching should be used to generate new openings.

Within nine months, Lynn had obtained an Advanced

Certificate in Counselling and Group work and become self-employed, finding plenty of work through the Social Services where she had previously been employed as a secretary. She also successfully completed a full-time postgraduate Diploma in Dramatherapy two years later and started her own professional practice as a dramatherapist providing services primarily for health authorities.

SEEKING PROFESSIONAL HELP

There is a great deal of professional advice available today for those seeking vocational guidance, and an increasing number of people are receiving career coaching from professional counsellors.

Skilled professionals can offer insights into your problems that friends or family can't provide. However, you must feel you are ready for career guidance to get the maximum benefit from it, and also be prepared to accept whatever it produces – both the good news and the bad.

The 'Outplacement' specialist

Outplacement firms are brought in by companies or organisations preparing to restructure themselves with the inevitable job losses that now seem to accompany this process. Reputable firms are staffed by qualified occupational psychologists and usually provide other services besides redundancy counselling, such as management development programmes, personal development and mid-career reviews. Some also provide services to individuals not sponsored by their company, but this can be expensive as fees are geared towards what an employer would be prepared to pay.

Outplacement arrived in the UK from the United States in the mid '70s as a way to help redundant executives. During the recession of the early 80s it was used to cater for the needs of more junior employees. Although outplacement services are still in the main for managerial and professional groups, there are some firms who provide guidance to other white-collar workers and also the semi-skilled manual worker.

The increased demand for their services has seen a dramatic

increase in the number of firms operating in the occupational psychology field. Although this means a greater choice, it has also meant the emergence of 'cowboy' operators, as anyone can claim to be a careers guidance adviser.

Occupational Guidance Advisers

The British Psychological Society (BPS), the recognised professional body for psychologists, maintains a *Directory of Chartered Psychologists* including those who provide vocational guidance. The directory is available at larger libraries and on the Society's website www.bps.org.uk. Any particular queries can be raised with the society. They can be contacted at:

> The British Psychological Society
> St Andrews House
> 48 Princess Road East
> Leicester LE1 7DR
> Tel: (0116) 254 9568
> Fax: (0116) 247 0787
> Email: enquiry@bps.org.uk

One firm which specialises in individual guidance for members of the public is Career Analysts in London. This firm, with its staff of well qualified occupational psychologists, has been established since 1965 and has a high reputation for providing sound vocational counselling at a reasonable cost to people of all ages from all over the British Isles. If you want further information on the range of services available, write to:

> Career Analysts
> Career House
> 90 Gloucester Place
> London W1U 6BL
> Tel: (020) 7935 5452
> Fax: (020) 7486 2211
> Email: info@careeranalysts.co.uk
> Website: www.careeranalysts.co.uk

There are other occupational or careers guidance advisers who

specialise in particular groups such as executives, managers or particular professions. These can be found on appointment pages in the national press, but you may wish to check what services they offer, the likely cost involved and the level of experience and expertise of their advisers before using them.

CHECKLIST

- If you are clear about the career you want to follow, what do you need to know about this career which you do not know at present?

- What sources of information will provide the answers?

- Are there any educational or experiential requirements which must be fulfilled before you can put your ideas into practice?

- If you need to acquire any additional qualifications, do you know what study options are available to you?

- What is the most appropriate method of study to meet your personal requirements?

- If you are not clear about what career you want to follow, what professional sources of help are available to you?

- What are the financial costs of seeking professional advice?

- Are you prepared to keep an open mind on the outcome?

- Are you committed to acting on the advice you are given?

- What do you understand is involved in achieving your new career?

Before moving on to Chapter 9, record your progress against Milestones 48–54 in Appendix 1, page 141.

9

Can I Afford It?

CAN I AFFORD TO TAKE THE PLUNGE?

'Affordability' in this chapter refers largely to the financial decisions facing you now you have decided what to do with your career. Whether you can afford to ignore your true motivational drives in terms of personal satisfaction has already been covered elsewhere.

It is a fact of life that whatever we decide to do, or not to do, it almost always comes down to finance. Can we afford to go on holiday? Can we afford a new car? Can we afford to re-decorate the house or to buy a new carpet? Sometimes, the choices can be more basic. Can we afford to pay the rent if we buy a joint of meat this week? Can we afford to buy the children new shoes if the gas bill comes early?

Getting into financial difficulties is a situation no-one should purposely set out to achieve. Nor should you go around pretending to yourself that it really doesn't matter. It does. Being short of cash can put an unbearable strain on even the most evenly balanced of relationships. You must never allow yourself to forget this if you have dependants whose well-being is in your hands. Be positive – but realistic. Don't set out on a course of action with half-formed ideas, and the vague hope that 'something will turn up'. It might not.

Why leave discussing the financial angle until now? – you might ask – especially if it is so important. The reason is simple. Until you know precisely what your plans are going to be, you cannot work out in detail the likely expenses involved; what funding might or might not be available; what additional financial help is on offer, and so on.

YOUR FINANCIAL INVENTORY

Existing outgoings

If you are out of work, no doubt you will have gone through your financial position with a fine tooth comb. If you are still working, however, this exercise is just as important. Be methodical.

1. **Make a list of all outstanding bills you have not paid and any credit card debts.** Your immediate aim should be to pay these off *as soon as possible*, particularly the outstanding amount on credit card statements. The interest rate on these is astronomical and you do yourself no favours by ignoring them. It would also be a wise move, until you are more certain of your financial future, to stick to cash or cheque transactions and to make sure any additional cardholder keeps to the same rules. If possible, pay off any hire purchase agreements you may have, especially those where non-payment could lead to a County Court judgement against you.

2. **Make a list of monthly outgoings for which you have been personally responsible up until now.** A suggested list is set out on pages 104 and 105. If you have annual expenses, divide these by twelve to produce a monthly figure. Deal with your quarterly bills by adding up the last four and dividing the total by twelve. Don't cut anything out at this stage until you have the complete pattern of spending in front of you, including any house maintenance costs you may have had to fund over the last year. Even though you don't expect these to be repeated, they will provide a buffer amount in your calculations for any other unexpected items you might have to fund in future.

3. **Make a separate list if a major item of family or domestic expenditure is regularly paid for by someone else (e.g. partner or parents).** Recording this expenditure is especially important if anything were to happen which resulted in this funding being discontinued and other

MONTHLY EXPENDITURE		
	Personal £	Other (name) £
House Mortgage/rent		
Building insurance		
Contents insurance		
Council tax		
Water rates		
Electricity		
Gas		
Telephone		
TV rental/licence		
Maintenance		
Replacements	_____	_____
	_____	_____
Housekeeping Basic food		
Drink		
Cleaning		
Laundry	_____	_____
	_____	_____
Travel Car loan repayments		
Tax/insurance		
Maintenance		
MOT		
Petrol		
Train fares		
Bus fares		
Hire charge	_____	_____
	_____	_____
Family costs School fees etc		
Clothing (children)		
Partner's allowance		
Children's pocket money		
Outstanding loans (list)		
....		
....		
Additional costs (state)		
....		
....	_____	_____
	_____	_____

Fig. 8. Budget for personal monthly expenditure.

Personal items	Insurance premiums	Personal £	Other (name) £
	....		
	....		
	....		
	Subscriptions (list)		
	....		
	....		
	....		
	Maintenance to former spouse/children		
	Savings schemes		
	Toiletries		
	Medicine		
	Dental charges		
	Clothes		
	Tobacco		
	Newspapers/magazines		
	Entertainment		
	Recreation/holiday costs		
	Birthday/Christmas expenses		
	Pocket money		
	Extras (specify)		
	....		
	....		

Add in 10% for cost of living increases
and unforeseen expenditure

GRAND TOTAL

monies had to be found to fill the gap. Death and divorce can happen, and it is unwise to place too much reliance on funds outside your immediate control.

The Grand Total represents the amount necessary to maintain your previous standard of living.

Present income
To counterbalance the outgoings, you need to know how much is coming in from all available sources, including any entitlement you might receive or be eligible for from social security in the form of allowances or pensions. As with your expenditure, use the month as the base and do any calculations which are necessary for comparison purposes.

• If you are receiving cash gifts from anyone as a general contribution to household expenses, make sure you note these down for the same reasons as mentioned earlier – you can't always take these gifts for granted.

• Suggested headings are set out on page 107.

FACING A SHORTFALL

Staying in control
The worst thing you can do if your new income level does not meet your potential level of expenditure is to pretend you don't have to face the problem. You do – even in the short term. Don't let things drift until you are in too deeply to get yourself out. Get yourself back onto an even keel as soon as possible. Tell *everyone* you owe money to that you are facing financial difficulties at the moment. The economic ups and downs of this country have ensured that there are a great many schemes now available to help those who are having trouble meeting their financial obligations. You may be facing only a short-term crisis, but you can't be sure. Plan for the long-term instead.

Consider doing some, if not all of the following:

• taking steps to re-schedule any loan debt or mortgage repayments

MONTHLY INCOME		
	Personal £	Other (name) £
Wages/salary (source)		
Interest		
Building Society		
Bank		
National Savings		
Dividends (name)		
Fees (source)		
Other income in cash (name source)	_____ _____	_____ _____
Jobseeker's allowance		
Social Security benefits		
Pensions (all sources)	_____ _____	_____ _____
GRAND TOTAL	_____ _____	_____ _____

Fig. 9. Budget for personal monthly income.

- informing the Council if you cannot keep up local tax payments

- contacting the gas or electricity companies etc if you are faced with a bill you can't meet immediately

- informing the court responsible for any maintenance order and the Child Support Agency to request adjustment of the amounts payable

- contacting your professional body to see if there are any arrangements for deferred or reduced subscription payments. **This is vital if you are in danger of losing your professional status through non-payment.**

Trying to muddle through may only make matters worse. You want to know that you can control your finances, especially if you intend to add into the calculations the complexities and expenses of retraining or returning to study. Don't expect to have all your problems solved by other people, however. It will be up to you to show you intend to play your own part by

- cutting back on your standard of living; or

- realising some of your assets.

Cutting back on your standard of living
This is not as easy as it sounds, but it may be the simplest option open to you in the short-term.

Before you ask everyone else in the household to tighten their belts however, look at your own list of items under 'Monthly Expenditure'. Identify those items you could personally:

- cut out absolutely
- cut down on a lot
- cut down on a little.

When you have trimmed your own life-style, you can perhaps expect others to show willing and follow suit.

Cutting back on others' standard of living

A partner who has come to rely on you as the breadwinner may
be genuinely unable to cope with the sudden reversal of
fortunes. Children brought up in an atmosphere of comparative
financial security don't always understand why they are
suddenly unable to have what they want when they want it, or
why some family activities have been drastically curtailed. An
elderly relative who has been relying on you to help out
financially here and there may find it difficult to come to terms
with the new reality. At a time when you are under considerable
stress yourself, you might find it hard to put yourself in their
shoes, but you will need to. You have to remember how it feels
when life starts to crumble around your ears. As far as your
family is concerned, the news will have exactly the same effect:
they no longer have control over their lives, and it can be very
frightening.

If you have been discussing and planning your future with
your partner and dependants, you will already know the extent
of their commitment to what you are trying to achieve. When it
comes to financial matters, you will need their wholehearted
support, particularly if you are facing a quite drastic
reorganisation of your lives. Keep talking and keep calm.

- Identify those areas of expenditure which have to be met to
  keep a roof over your heads, and everyone warm, fed and
  clothed. After that, it's a matter of questioning the need to
  continue spending under every other heading and pruning
  out the non-essentials.

- Try to keep up the important insurance payments, for
  instance, but let 'the icing on the cake' policies lapse. Cut
  out luxury items. Choose less expensive alternatives under
  priority headings, provided these are just as good value for
  money.

- Look at other areas. Do you really need the use of a car for
  instance? Would it make better financial sense in your case
  to use public transport and taxis taking into account rising
  fuel costs, tax, insurance and servicing?

Realising your assets

This is an option which may become necessary in the longer term.

1. **List all the items available to you which you could sell if necessary.** Possible headings are set out on pages 110 and 111.
2. **Deduct from the valuation any loan debts that might be outstanding.** Don't forget the deferred payments on the car or PC package.
3. **Note any variation in your outgoings which the disposal of the item would represent in your monthly/annual expenditure.** Selling a piece of jewellery might reduce your insurance premiums. Selling your home would replace monthly repayments with rental charges.
4. **Consult properly qualified professionals or experts for property and other valuables.** If you are thinking of selling the car, check with a reputable motor dealer on the current state of the second-hand car market.

Some of the items on your list will have a fluctuating value, so be prepared to revise this information at regular intervals to keep your financial picture as up-to-date as possible. It may be prudent to sell an item sooner rather than later if the market is buoyant, or defer a sale if it is in the doldrums.

It is worth remembering that household furniture and electrical goods have very little second-hand value if you are making a forced sale. By the time you have taken off the cost of removal and the saleroom commission, you are likely to come away with only a few pounds in your pocket. Make sure it is worth disposing of these assets first.

The same applies if you have to realise some of your investments. Make yourself aware of the benefit which accrues from each of them before parting with them.

- Is the benefit a safety net for the future?

- Does the investment provide regular income?

	AVAILABLE ASSETS		
	Valuation	Less outstanding debt if sold	Variation on monthly expenditure if sold
	£	£	£
House			
Furniture			
Car(s)			
. . . .			
Other properties			
. . . .			
. . . .			
Caravan/boat			
Electrical goods			
Music system			
Computer(s)			
TV(s)			
Other			
. . . .			
. . . .			
Jewellery			
. . . .			
. . . .			

Fig. 10. Inventory of assets and investments.

INVESTMENTS			
	Value	Date of maturity	Loss of monthly income if sold
	£		£
Stocks and shares			
. . . .			
. . . .			
Bank accounts			
. . . .			
. . . .			
Building Society accounts			
. . . .			
. . . .			
Premium bonds			
National Savings Certificates			
. . . .			
. . . .			
Other (name)			
. . . .			
. . . .			
Insurance policies (name)			
. . . .			
. . . .			
Total	——		——

Fig. 10. continued

You may have to consider sacrificing the safety net to bolster your present finances. If you do this, you will have to gamble on there being time enough when finances improve to replace the net at a later date.

CHOICES WHEN RETHINKING AN OLD CAREER

There is a good chance that if you are intending to re-enter the job market using your old skills in a new way, once you know what way this is, you will not be out of a job too long. The situation becomes a little more difficult if you need to update your skills, and a lot more difficult if you know your job-search is going to involve looking at locations away from your present home base.

Will you need to move?
It is generally accepted that moving house is one of the top three most stressful life experiences, along with death and divorce.

It is also expensive. You have to allow for some or all of the following:

- legal fees (buying and selling)

- stamp duty

- estate agents' fees

- local search charges

- removal costs

- replacement costs (carpets and curtains)

- hidden extras.

If you find yourself having to move without selling your old house, you also have to make allowances for paying two mortgages, financing a bridging loan and, if the house remains unsold after six months, continuing to pay council tax on the unoccupied property, all of which are a huge drain on your resources.

Is the new area more expensive?

If you are thinking of moving to another area, get a copy of a local paper and compare house prices with the location you are already living in. Adverts by some of the larger retailers will also give you some idea as to local cost of living. Contact the local council as well and ask about the level of council tax for the area. All these costs can fluctuate widely in a relatively small geographical area.

Will you need to commute?

This may be an alternative to full scale relocation. It may be preferable if children are reaching a critical time in their education or if your partner is established in a well-paid job. The costs involved in commuting can be expensive. Don't underestimate these or the cost in terms of your personal energy level, your loss of leisure time or your availability to meet family commitments.

Will your new salary match your old?

It may not if you are consciously readjusting your status level downwards, or having to take a less responsible position until you have retrained or taken additional qualifications.

Make sure you are able to restructure your financial arrangements to take account of this, either in the short-term until you are fully qualified, or on a longer-term basis if you are not aiming for the more high-powered type of job.

Are there financial implications in retraining?

If you are required to update your skills or take additional qualifications as part of your new job, check with your employer what financial help is available from the firm to off-set any costs such as tuition fees or equipment. If you have to find the finance yourself, you need to be certain you can put the funding together. Find out too whether there are any financial or other penalties if you want to take a course which is during the working day. Your employers may expect you to update your skills in your own time at your own expense.

CHOICES WHEN STARTING FROM SCRATCH

What are the financial implications of retraining?
There will *always* be some financial outlay or pressure on existing finances if you are starting from scratch. Retraining costs money, whether you are embarking on a course of study to obtain a new qualification, or having to work out your time in a lesser role to gain the necessary experience. Affordability has a major role to play.

Affordability in this context means not only the financial implications of retraining but also the necessary input of both time and personal commitment you will need to sink into your project, and all the ramifications this can have on your own life and those around you.

Expenses involved in taking a formal course include amongst other things such items as:

- tuition fees

- books and equipment

- accommodation charges if you are living away from home

- supporting the family home if you are resident on campus

- travelling costs.

These items alone can add up to a formidable sum, so you must be sure you can meet them as well as your existing commitments.

How can I finance my college studies?
There are many ways open to you depending on a whole range of requirements by different grant-making bodies. For instance, financial assistance may depend on:

- whether you are a full-time or part-time student
- whether you have received grant-aid in the past
- the level of the course you are taking
- the college offering the course
- the method of study you intend to adopt

- the area of study you want to pursue
- your age
- a means test.

And so on. The following are just some of the avenues which might be open to you.

Maintenance costs and tuition fees

It is almost impossible to give across the board advice on this topic: so much depends on where a student is living or studying; the type of course being undertaken; whether financial assistance has been given in the past and what is available for an adult learner rather than someone who has just left school. If you don't have access to the Internet, your best course of action is to contact your nearest Learning and Skills Council, JobCentre Plus office or regional government department. Your local library and benefits office might also have useful leaflets available.

If you have access to the Internet and live in England, the best site to get you started is probably www. direct.gov.uk/Education AndLearning which has a section dealing with financial assistance for adult learners. This includes internal links to career development loans, grants, bursaries and funding in general for higher education. There are also links to sections on financing your learning, free courses for adults and adult learning grants as well as external links on information about help with the cost of learning, searching for funding and money to learn.

The Welsh Assembly has expanded its range of student support over recent years, so if you are living in Wales it might be useful to contact:

The Department for Education and Lifelong Learning
National Assembly for Wales
Cardiff Bay
Cardiff CF99 1NA
Tel: (029) 2082 5111
Website: www.wales.gov.uk

In Scotland contact:

> The Scottish Executive Education Department
> Victoria Quay
> Edinburgh EH6 6QQ
> Tel: (0131) 556 8400
> Website: www.scotland.gov.uk

In Northern Ireland you should contact:

> The Department for Employment and Learning
> Adelaide House
> 39-49 Adelaide Street
> Belfast
> BT2 8FD
> Tel: (028) 9025 7777
> Website: www.delni.gov.uk

Learner Support Funds

These are limited funds distributed by colleges to provide help to students who face serious financial difficulties, or where access to higher education might be inhibited by financial problems. Further information can also be obtained from the Student Support or Student Services Office of the college you hope to attend, who are also responsible for administering the fund.

Grants and bursaries

In England, provision of financial assistance in the form of grants rather than loans is now dependent on government initiatives aimed at particular sections of the community. To find out more about whether you would qualify, contact the Learning and Skills Council covering the area of your course provider, or check out the Adult Learning section on the Education and Learning page of the Directgov website to see what is currently available.

There are educational charities and trusts who make grants towards the costs of studying. These are listed in *The Grants Register* which can be found in larger libraries but you can also

contact the Educational Grants Advisory Service (EGAS) which provides advice on funding for post-16 students in the UK. The address is:

> Educational Grants Advisory Service
> The Family Welfare Association
> 501-505 Kingsland Road
> Dalston
> London E8 4AU
> Telephone Helpline: (020) 7254 6251
> Website: www.egas-online.org

Bursaries are similar to grants inasmuch as you do not have to repay any monies made available to you. They are usually linked to particular professions or qualifications such as teacher training or NHS roles. Your training provider, trades union, professional body or potential employer should be able to provide you with advice on what is available and how to apply. There are also useful links to access information on bursaries on the Directgov website.

If you are studying as part of your status as a trainee with an organisation, check with the training officer what expenses are going to be paid for by the firm.

Personal loans from banks

There are loan packages on offer from the High Street banks both for first time students and those taking further study or postgraduate courses. The packages vary considerably from bank to bank so it is worth shopping around to see what is on offer and which would suit you best.

Career Development Loans

These loans are available through some high street banks providing a deferred repayment scheme for the duration of your course. The interest is paid by the Learning and Skills Council for this period and up to one month afterwards. The loan is then repaid to the bank over an agreed period at a fixed rate of interest.

Career Development Loans have been operating for many

years now, but the administration arrangements, the amounts available and the banks participating in the scheme do vary over time. To see what is available currently either contact your local Learning Skills Council or look on the Career Development Loans page of the Directgov website. The latter also gives useful links to other information and contacts.

Full-time or part-time work
There may be no alternative open to you but to complete your studies in your own time and finance them from employment. This employment may not have any connection with what you are studying: it may simply be a means of funding your studies and keeping yourself financially secure. If you are expected to have a certain level of practical experience in your new career as well as a formal qualification, however, it would obviously make sense to obtain some form of related employment.

Savings
If the worst comes to the worst and there is absolutely no other way of funding your new start, you may have to consider digging into your savings. Obviously, you have to be absolutely sure you are not jeopardising your financial security to the point of no return by doing so.

State benefits
Social security provision is complex and subject to rapid change. If you want to be certain of your entitlement you would be better advised to make an appointment at your nearest office and talk through your particular circumstances with a member of the staff.

You will find the nearest office in *The Phone Book* under the full page entry for Jobcentre Plus.

Friends and relations
You may be able to turn to close friends or relatives who might be prepared to give you some financial backing. Before accepting help however, be absolutely certain you understand whether you are receiving a gift or a loan. If it is a loan, then make sure you know the basis on which it is being given. Better still, put it down in writing so that both parties agree.

What are the financial implications of needing additional experience?

Needing experience as well as being properly qualified can be an additional financial hurdle to cross. You may be able to obtain the necessary expertise as part of your course, but where this is not possible you may have to consider the following:

1. Applying for low-status or trainee posts in the first instance.
2. Taking part-time jobs in relevant fields during your vacations.
3. Taking a 'filler' full-time job and taking on voluntary work in your spare time in your new sphere of activity if this is appropriate.

Whichever avenue you take, there will be some financial impact in both the short- and long-term. Calculate what this will be and what adjustments might be necessary in your financial arrangements. Be prepared to do whatever is necessary to achieve your objective, but always bear in mind your need to maintain financial security.

Case study: Discovering financial ways and means

Gill Brown was a frustrated actress working as a temporary secretary to pay the mortgage of her small London flat. She had not been successful in securing a part for a very long time and was becoming increasingly bitter. This bitterness was beginning to affect her behaviour: she was becoming more remote and very snappy with her colleagues.

Outside her work she vented her anger by joining pressure groups and campaigning for change. She composed lots of letters to influential people and began to get feedback from several sources that she was very good at this – in fact much better than many lawyers used by the campaigns in the past. This fired her imagination and she began to wonder if she could make the transition from actress to lawyer.

Gill already had a degree in English and was eligible to take a one year Law conversion course. However, she would also have to complete a further year at Bar School and then a year's pupillage as a junior barrister without any income.

She talked the problem over with her bank manager and was surprised to find the bank offered career development loans. Aged 38, she applied to law school and was given a place. The bank gave her £15,000 over two years which helped to cover her household expenses, the loan to be repaid at a low interest rate over a six year period.

Gill then won a scholarship from the Middle Temple for £8,000 as a female mature entrant. This helped to pay for the course fees and books and was not repayable. Additional small donations from charities also went towards the cost of purchasing books. By converting to vegetarian food, she was able to eat well but more cheaply, and by buying good winter clothes from charity shops, she was also able to keep down the level of her personal expenditure.

Her parents provided a financial safety net to help with emergencies and to give her a break from the very hard and intense study routine.

Gill passed all her exams and gained the 12 month pupillage with a group of barristers specialising in criminal law. Her prospects now look very good and the sacrifices she made in the past are more than compensated for by the rewards she can look forward to in the future.

CHECKLIST

- Can you sustain your previous standard of living? If not, what areas have you identified which will need to be pruned?

- Have you taken steps to pay off outstanding debts and informed everyone who should know of your changed financial circumstances?

- What assets could you realise if necessary?

- What are the financial implications of moving house? Is commuting a viable and cheaper alternative?

- What are the short- and long-term financial implications of what you intend to do?

- What are the costs involved in returning to study?

- How do you propose to finance these?

- What costs are likely to be involved in obtaining any additional experience you need for your new career?

- How do you intend to finance these?

- Are there other less costly or less disruptive ways to achieve your retraining objectives?

Before moving on to Chapter 10, record your progress against Milestones 55–62 in Appendix 1, page 142.

10

Stepping Out

WHAT NOW?

Not everything works out the way we expect it will. The best laid plans go awry. At the end of the last chapter, we considered the possibility of having to come to terms with being unable to reach our goal, for whatever reason.

Frustration and disappointment, even anger perhaps, will cloud your judgement if you let them. Don't. This applies whether you know right from the outset that you can't do what you most want to, or whether you meet obstacles on the way to your new career that stand between you and success. Your determination to succeed will carry you far, but it may not carry you all the way. Be prepared for setbacks along the road and try not to let them overwhelm you. Yes, it is easier said than done, but being positive can often solve seemingly insoluble problems. Be flexible in your approach, or tackle the problem in a different way.

COMING TO TERMS WITH OBSTACLES

Right from the start

If you find there is absolutely no way you can move forward either immediately or in the foreseeable future don't despair. Although you may find it difficult to convince yourself, you are now in a far better position to control your prospects than you were before you started putting together your Self Portrait. For instance, you now know your greatest strengths, your preferences, the best working environment to suit your individual personality, and which motivational drives carry you forward.

If you have no way of starting a new career, then decide how to make the best of a bad situation by *using what you know about yourself as a guideline.*

If you need to change the content of your working life – say from the indoor to the outdoor – don't push yourself back into work situations which you now know are totally unsuitable. Shift the emphasis of your old career, so that what you are looking for in a job fits your personal needs and preferences better.

If you are faced with a complete mis-match between your motivational drives and your previous career, then aim to minimise the main areas of conflict. For instance, don't apply for jobs which involve team work or high-powered activity if you are at your best working on your own or prefer the quiet, steady sort of life. Once again, shift the emphasis. Find a way round the aspects you found most irritating, or nerve-racking, by careful selection.

Most important of all, you will need to find personal fulfilment outside the working day. This means looking for the type of job which has precise conditions of employment with no commitment to put in additional hours either in the workplace itself or by taking work home. Your personal spare time is precious. You need to allow your 'real' self the chance to develop and flourish through your leisure activities.

Most jobs which are undemanding are likely to be fairly mundane, unglamorous and out of the mainstream of promotional activity. By aiming for this type of job you are making your working life a means to an end, and not an end in itself.

This situation can put you in something of a dilemma: you cannot hope to succeed at an interview if you do not show at least some basic enthusiasm for the job you have applied for. So how can you be enthusiastic about a job which is simply a means of earning a living? Precisely because it is just that: it gives you the security of providing for yourself and your dependants while at the same time giving you the freedom to develop and extend your potential away from the workplace. The content of the job, or its future potential, is not as important as the financial security and personal space it offers.

There are two other likely consequences to take into account:

1. **A potential drop in your standard of living either immediately or in the future**. Make sure your dependants understand why you have made your decision to take the slow lane. As you have probably had to give up any ideas of a new career to safeguard their financial security, your commitment to them should not be in question. If you have been talking through your ideas and including everyone in the decision-making processes, it is not unreasonable to hope that you receive their support.

2. **A happier, healthier retirement**. Too many people who make work their whole life suffer from ill-health or premature death within the first year after retirement. By making life outside the workplace the central feature of your existence, statistically you are more likely to survive to a ripe old age with your energy and mental vigour intact and be far better placed to make better use of your increased number of non-working years.

The short-term hiccup

Even if you can see your way to making a start on your new career, you may not be able to get off the starting blocks immediately. There are all sorts of reasons which might prevent you from putting your plans into immediate effect.

- You may have to wait for the beginning of a new academic year.

- Your finances may not be what they should be immediately but the prospects look brighter in six months' time.

- You may need to get some practical experience under your belt before you can apply for a particular course.

Under these circumstances, how should you tackle the gap?

Whatever you do, don't lose your initial enthusiasm for the enterprise by lack of action. If you are still employed but waiting for the beginning of a new academic year, contact the college and find out what background reading material would be useful to give you a head start. If you haven't been able to commit

yourself to a course until your finances improve, do the same.
Or if you need practical experience, contact someone who is
actively involved in the area of work you hope to train in. Ask if
they would be prepared to let you 'shadow' them during a
working period if this is appropriate.

If you are out of a job, aim if you can for a 'filler' that will
be useful to you in your future career, or if this is not possible,
keep yourself involved in your project outside the workplace
by taking on activities to bolster your enthusiasm, whether this
is by reading or practical experience, by shadowing or
involvement with voluntary work. Always keep your long-term
aim in mind.

The long-term strategy

You may be faced with the prospect of being unable to start
retraining for your new career for some time. Perhaps you will
have to wait several years until the children have left school, or
until the mortgage is paid for, or your partner completes a
course of study. Perhaps you simply need more time to get your
finances into better shape.

Sustaining enthusiasm over the long-term requires
concentrated effort and a strategy designed to boost your spirits
so that you never lose sight of your goal over the long interval
between initial determination and putting this into effect.

Planning is the all important feature of your strategy.

- Set a specific date when you intend to make the break and
  start your new career.

- Set up milestones in the interval between by which time
  you expect to meet certain targets, such as paying off the
  mortgage or completing a foundation course by distance
  learning modules.

- Scale down your financial commitments gradually if there
  is going to be a strain on your budget during your retraining
  period.

- Revise your personal life-style over the intervening months
  so that you can adapt to your changed circumstances more

easily when the time comes.

- If possible, join the group or body which represents people in your new sphere of work and keep abreast of developments taking place in this field.

- As with the short-term hiccup, try to obtain employment in some way connected with your new career, or arrange to shadow a potential future colleague.

- Subscribe to any publications which might provide useful information.

- Nearer the time when you intend to make the break, make a start on essential course reading.

Some parts of your plan may need to be flexible. Don't make it so rigid that any failure to meet a particular deadline becomes a crisis. Starting a new career is traumatic enough without adding unnecessary stress to the situation.

PLANNING THE JOB SEARCH

Whether you are looking for a 'filler' job, a new job in your old career, or a position in your completely new career, carry out your job search with equal care and attention to detail. You now know who you are, what you are, and what you do best under which conditions, and this gives you a head start on most candidates if you use this information properly. Don't waste this precious knowledge by sloppy job-hunting.

There is still the awful tendency if you have been under financial pressure for some time to slip back into old habits by starting to apply for anything and everything which looks vaguely hopeful.

DON'T use the scatter-gun approach to job-hunting.
DO target the most appropriate jobs and no others.

Using the scatter-gun approach

If you are going to aim at every job which you *might* be able to do then you have wasted your time completing your Self

Portrait and identifying your ideal work environment. The reason you completed these exercises was to help you make better use of your opportunity to find new employment. Blasting away at anything that moves is:

– wasteful of energy and effort
– expensive on postage and paper
– depressing because of the high failure rate
– unlikely to lead to success for the right reasons.

When you apply for a job you are saying to a prospective employer – This is Me. This is what I have done. This is what I am good at. This is how I think I will be good at the job you have on offer – and you have to be convincing, not only to the prospective employer, but to yourself. When you apply for a job, you have to be certain it is *the right job for you.*

STOP AND THINK if you find yourself picking out jobs from the situations vacant columns on the basis of the 'I suppose I *might* be able to do that' theory. Yes, you might. You might even be able to convince your potential employer that you might. All you are really doing, however, is fooling yourself and everyone else.

If you manage to get a job on this basis you face three possibilities:

1.   Your unsuitability for the job becomes evident to everyone which can ultimately lead to dismissal.

2.   You discover your own shortcomings and decide you have to find alternative employment.

3.   You discover your own shortcomings but struggle on miserably because you can't face the trauma of being out of work.

None of these outcomes is desirable. They don't improve your self-image, your self-development, or your career history on future application forms.

Aiming at the most appropriate jobs

Depending on what you are looking for, there are several sources of information you can use in your job search.

Jobcentre
If you are looking for local employment in basic office work, catering, retailing, openings in the building trade and associated crafts, the Jobcentre is a good beginning.

Local papers
Again, a good source for local employment with the benefit of a wider range of job opportunities from the manual through to the manager.

National press
Advertising space in the national dailies is expensive. Firms and organisations who take space are therefore hoping to reach a wider readership and attract a good response. The ads are usually for the better paid job with attractive career prospects.

Most national dailies set aside specific days for particular career vacancies, but these do not coincide with one another and each paper operates a different approach. Some jobs appear under general listings in some papers. In others, they come under a specific category which is carried on one particular day of the week. In some cases, more senior posts belonging to the same category are published on a different day to the more junior positions. You have to keep your eyes open for the variations. And it doesn't end there. With the ebb and flow of demand in the jobs market, the national dailies vary their format over the passage of time. So you have to be clear about which papers and which editions are the most useful for you to study. Check which days are relevant for your job search to save spending money on unnecessary editions. If you are close to a library, drop in on the appropriate day and scour their copies. The quality broadsheets also have their own appointments websites on the Net.

Internet
The rapid expansion of the Internet has resulted in hundreds of

recruitment websites, many providing much more information than simple lists of vacancies. Some include sections on job seeking and CV writing as well as articles on topics such as career change. Like all websites however, it is not always clear how up-to-date the entries are. Individual companies and organisations are also increasingly opening up their own vacancies websites to attract applicants, and if you have specific employers in mind, accessing their websites may be a more worthwhile exercise.

If you are still in employment, however, it is important to be aware that your use of the Net for job-hunting purposes can be picked up by your employer if you use computer facilities in the workplace. You could find yourself in an embarrassing situation as a result.

Professional publications
These are an obvious choice if you have a specific profession in mind. They are often published by the nationally recognised controlling organisation or association for that profession so they also contain articles and features which keep you up to date with the latest thinking and good practices.

Voluntary work
This is especially useful if you are aiming for a career in some sort of caring capacity. Voluntary agencies usually have excellent contacts with paid professionals through both formal and informal meetings. These offer you the opportunity to 'put yourself about', to make yourself visible to people who might have a say in recruitment, and to make enquiries about likely openings which might be available in the future. If you are seen to be doing a good job as a voluntary worker, your chances of being absorbed into the paid workforce are greatly improved.

Personal contacts
Never underestimate the value of these. You do not have to debase yourself or appear to be a 'creep' by making use of the inside information that friends or potential colleagues either offer you or are prepared to give if they are asked. Do not necessarily expect them to put in a good word for you as they

may not feel this is appropriate, but they may be able to tell you about potential openings which you might not otherwise know existed, or advise you to take a particular course of action to help your application stand out above the rest.

MAKING APPLICATIONS

This is a subject in itself. If you are a bit rusty on the techniques of putting together a good application and getting the best out of job interviews, don't neglect this part of the process. It's crucial.

Regardless of what sort of job you are applying for, you could waste all your previous time and effort by sloppy or inadequate presentation. It's no good being the best person for the job if everything else about you implies that you are not.

Briefly, there are three areas you must concentrate on if you are to succeed in getting a job in a competitive job market:

1. Thorough research of both the job you are applying for and the organisation which would be employing you.

2. Proper emphasis in your application to show you can match the skills being sought.

3. Effective personal presentation at all points of contact with your potential employer, whether this is in the written form, on the phone, or at an interview.

Researching the job and organisation

Employers are looking for someone who not only fits the bill as far as the job is concerned, but also someone who is interested in the organisation. This is especially true in larger concerns and those with a good career structure. But even small-scale firms often want to see potential employees being interested in working for them rather than their competitors.

An applicant who gives the impression he or she has weighed up the alternatives and decided to apply for a position with a particular firm is giving the strongest signal of all – I like you. It is a natural reaction in everyone to like other people who like us – and recruiters are no different in this respect.

Effective personal presentation

In writing

It should go without saying that anything written to your potential future employer should be legible, coherent and well set out. This applies to letters, application forms or your curriculum vitae.

They should be informative, concise and precise. Anything more will be a turn-off, particularly to a busy personnel officer who might be sifting through hundreds of similar applications.

If your standard of handwriting is poor, then arrange for written work to be typed. Beware of printed application forms which do not conform to standard typing spaces. The effect of a badly typed form is as negative as a badly written one. In these circumstances, you are better advised to develop your own style of clear printing for use on application forms only.

On the phone

Before you make contact, know who you want to speak to and be prepared to be referred to someone else if your initial point of contact is not available. Know what you want to say – and say it – nothing else. Make sure if someone takes a message that you give them all the information necessary to pass on the correct information.

Just like your written work, your phone calls should be informative, concise and precise.

At interview

If you have not had the experience of an interview for some time, brush up on your technique. It could let you down. This applies too if you have had several interviews but no successes to date. Your presentation might be what's at fault, not your qualifications to do a good job.

There are a whole range of books available both at booksellers and libraries to help you improve your interview performance. Before choosing which one is right for you however, check whether it is written for the UK or the US market. US interviewing techniques are substantially different from those adopted by most recruiters in the UK. Unless you intend to work for a US firm, the advice offered by these books

is likely to give you a distorted view of what to expect from an interview, and encourage you in adopting the sort of approach which would not necessarily meet with universal approval here.

SPECIAL PROBLEMS FOR CAREER CHANGERS

Persuading potential employers or financial backers to take you seriously

If you are branching out into an entirely new field, your main problem is to convince other people who need to be convinced that you aren't just taking a leap into the dark. To do this, your application, whether this is for a job or financial backing, *must* bring out the following points:

- your transferable or portable skills
- your willingness to train or retrain
- any evidence of preliminary training already undertaken
- any evidence of leisure activities which support your decision to change careers
- any evidence of current experience, such as voluntary work, shadowing or temporary employment in a similar or related field, which supports your application
- any professional references to back up your decision to take a new career direction
- anything else which might add credence to your decision.

Pitfalls to avoid

Dwelling on the past

The major problem you have to overcome is the tendency to concentrate on your previous misfortune. This is very easily done if you have had to struggle to readjust your life or make the best of a bad job in coming to terms with your future.

Applications riddled with negative words and phrases such as 'unfortunately'. 'I was unable to . . .'. 'I failed . . .' and the like are an immediate turn off. Avoid them like the plague. Applications must be positive and optimistic – but not over-optimistic. Choose your words carefully, reread what you have written and ask yourself what impression you are giving.

The all-purpose curriculum vitae
It is tempting to draw up your CV, run off a string of photocopies and use it rather like a standard letter whenever a CV is requested. This is fine if you are aiming at a broad range of similar jobs. If you are targeting a specific post, however, an all-purpose CV is less likely to bring out the qualities you want to emphasise the most. This is especially true when you are changing careers.

An explanatory covering letter might serve to clarify matters, but you are gambling on the willingness of a busy personnel officer to study additional material, the possibility of your explanation being overlooked, or the potential for the letter to become separated from your CV and be lost.

It may take longer to prepare, but you would be better advised to shape your CV to match the requirements of each particular job. Keep it to a single sheet of A4 and reduce your covering letter to the basic point of telling the reader which job you are applying for. Once your application is in the correct pile, it no longer matters if the covering letter becomes detached. Use this more focused approach too if you are applying for jobs using Internet recruitment sites.

If you are unsure of how to produce a good CV, borrow or buy a book on the subject and learn how to present yourself to the best of your ability in as concise and attractive a manner as possible.

Remember, you owe it both to yourself and to those who depend on you to succeed in your new career. More and more people are doing just that.

CHECKLIST

- If you are faced with being unable to make a change in your career, what plans have you made to continue your self-development away from the workplace?

- If you are unable to start on your new career immediately, what strategies do you intend to adopt to keep your enthusiasm alive in the short-term?

- If you are having to accept it will be some time before you can start your new career, what is your long-term strategy to help you achieve your goal?

- What events could alter the timescale of your strategy and in what way?

- What sources of information have you identified as being the best ones for the type of job you are looking for?

- What selection criteria are you adopting when studying job vacancy notices? Are these appropriate to your needs?

- What sources of information are available to you to carry out background research into the job on offer and the organisation offering it?

- What areas of your personal presentation do you feel you need to brush up on and how do you intend to do this?

- What aspects of your experience, skills or ability do you feel it is important to stress in your job application?

- What aspects, if any, of your career history do you feel should play a less important role?

Record the completion of Milestones 63–70 in Appendix 1, pages 142–143.

Appendix 1:
Personal Milestones,
a Career Diary

Part 1 – Data Gathering

		Relevant dates	
		Completed	*Revised*
1	Review of why you want to change your career.	_____	_____
2	Research of job market and employment trends.	_____	_____
3	Completion of family background questionnaire.	_____	_____
4	Completion of personal details questionnaire.	_____	_____
5	Review of family influences/ traumas/ experiences.	_____	_____
6	Completion of education, training and achievements questionnaire.	_____	_____
7	Review of educational influences/achievements.	_____	_____
8	Completion of present family questionnaire.	_____	_____
9	Completion of working history and experience questionnaire.	_____	_____

		Relevant dates	
		Completed	*Revised*

10 Review of your first full-time employment.

11 Review of subsequent jobs.

12 Identification of what you liked most/least about a job.

13 Identification of which job you enjoyed most and why.

14 Brainstorming what you would like to do.

15 Identification of possible career openings based on 14.

16 Identification of what might be stopping you from doing these.

17 Identification of ways in which any hurdles might be overcome.

18 Completion of hobbies and interests questionnaire.

19 Compilation of a list of personal initiatives.

20 Completion of your present interests questionnaire.

21 Review of the social context of your hobbies and interests.

22 Identification of your favourite spare time interest.

	Relevant dates	
	Completed	*Revised*

23 Review of the motivational drives
     behind your spare time interests. _____   _____

24 Translation of these motivational
     drives into desirable qualities in
     the workplace.   _____   _____

25 Completion of fictitious job
     advertisement seeking these
     qualities.   _____   _____

26 Review of your various life roles
     within the family.   _____   _____

27 Review of roles in the working
     environment.   _____   _____

28 Review of roles in the non-
     working environment.   _____   _____

29 Review of your self-image.   _____   _____

30 Identification of any aspects of
     your image you would want to
     change.   _____   _____

Part II – Using the Data

31 Identification of the right working
     environment for you.   _____   _____

32 Review of the effect of the
     influence of your personality
     factors and motivational drives
     on your choice of future career.   _____   _____

33 Identification of the full range of
     your skills and abilities.   _____   _____

	Relevant dates	
	Completed	*Revised*

34 Identification of the preferred level of responsibility in your work environment. _____   _____

35 Identification of the preferred social mix in your work environment. _____   _____

36 Completion of the job description of your 'perfect' job. _____   _____

37 Identification of the type of job you want to avoid. _____   _____

Part III – Rethinking the Old Career

38 Review and restatement of why you want to change your career. _____   _____

39 Review of preferred level of responsibility. _____   _____

40 Review of existing commitments. _____   _____

41 Identification of which stereotype matches your present circumstances. _____   _____

42 Identification of preferred size of organisation in the work environment. _____   _____

43 Identification of any preferred change of status in the work environment. _____   _____

Relevant dates

Completed   *Revised*

44 Identification of preferred working
environment.

45 Review of possible work
locations outside your immediate
area.

46 Review of skills base.

47 Identification of any retraining
requirements.

Part IV – Breaking New Ground

48 Identification of what you want to
do.

49 Identification of what level you
want to aim for.

50 Identification of preferred working
environment.

51 Identification of any additional
facets you want to see in your
new job.

52 Identification of what retraining is
needed.

53 Review of methods and financing
of any essential retraining.

54 Identification of job opportunities
in your chosen field.

| | **Relevant dates** | |
| | *Completed* | *Revised* |

Part V – Finance

55 Completion of your monthly
expenditure questionnaire.

56 Completion of your monthly
income questionnaire.

57 Review of your financial
situation.

58 Completion of your available
assets questionnaire.

59 Completion of your investments
questionnaire.

60 Identification of costs involved in
relocating.

61 Identification of financial
implications of retraining.

62 Identification of sources of
additional funding.

Part VI – Planning the Future

63 Completion of short-term
strategy.

64 Completion of longer-term
strategy.

65 Completion of application to
college.

Relevant dates

	Completed	*Revised*
66 Identification of appropriate 'filler' jobs.	_____	_____
67 Preparation of appropriate CV.	_____	_____
68 Review of personal presentation in a job hunting situation.	_____	_____
69 Identification of any areas needing improvement.	_____	_____
70 Identification of time-scale when data will need to be reviewed.	_____	_____

Appendix 2
Personal Directory

Description	Contact Name	Tel/email/website
Jobcentre	. . . .	. . . .
Library	. . . .	. . . .
Training Provider	. . . .	. . . .
Local LSC	. . . .	. . . .
College or University	. . . .	. . . .
Student Support or Student Services Office	. . . .	. . . .
National Office of Professional Association or Body	. . . .	. . . .
Local Office of Professional Association or Body	. . . .	. . . .
Careers Guidance Specialist	. . . .	. . . .
Bank	. . . .	. . . .
Social Security Office	. . . .	. . . .
Other	. . . .	. . . .
. . . .	. . . .	. . . .
. . . .	. . . .	. . . .
Useful websites	. . . .	
	. . . .	

Appendix 3
Additional Case Studies:
Turning Hobbies into Careers

Catherine Gray (28) – Single

Catherine had always been interested in the Arts and her hobbies included collecting antiques and restoration. She took a Diploma in Secretarial Duties and the Liberal Arts but was unable to focus on which career to follow. Eventually, she took up employment in an estate agency.

Feeling she had made the wrong choice she consulted an occupational psychologist. Her assessment tests confirmed that her strongest interests lay in the Arts and it was suggested she should take a course in the Applied Arts and Interior Design.

More confident in her approach, Catherine followed up the suggestion and completed a course in the History of Art, gaining employment with one of the larger auction houses as well as doing research for the Victorian Picture Department with the ultimate goal of becoming an expert.

Mary Bullen (32) – Single

Mary had a variety of hobbies, but her main interests lay in cookery and nutrition. She had completed a languages degree at university and then a course for the bi-lingual secretary. Her working record however was symptomatic of having made the wrong choice at university. Her jobs included a succession of short-term commitments as secretary, courier and waitress, amongst others.

Career guidance highlighted Mary's desire to escape from a desk-bound job and to maximise the interest she had in cookery. She was advised to take a good quality cookery course with the aim of running her own restaurant at some stage in the future.

Mary followed up the advice and completed a Diploma in Vegetarian Cookery and subsequently gained employment as a chef.

Ann Stuart (18) – Single

Ann had completed her A-Levels and was about to start a Foundation Course at Art School when she lost confidence in what she was doing. Her main spare time interest was voluntary work on a playscheme with handicapped children and she was beginning to think she should be considering a more care orientated career.

Her career counsellor was able to suggest the amalgamation of both interests by following up the Foundation Course with a Fine Arts Degree and then a postgraduate course in Primary School Teaching and Art Therapy. Ann embarked on this course of action whilst still keeping in touch with her voluntary work and was able to feel far more confident about her future.

Diane Matthews (29) – Married

Diane's parents were both very academically inclined and encouraged her to follow in their footsteps. Diane was equally as gifted and eventually she obtained a PhD in Biochemistry going on to become a research scientist herself.

Diane's hobbies, however, were in stark contrast to the 'blue-stocking' image of her profession. She loved sports and was particulary keen on hot-air ballooning which she was very good at. Gradually, she began to realise that the life of a research scientist was not for her.

Career guidance highlighted the mis-match between Diane's work environment and her true motivational drives and interests. It was suggested that she should consider taking a business qualification with a view to moving eventually into the recreation and leisure field.

Having accrued a reasonable savings buffer during her working life, Diane decided to take the plunge and planned to resign her post and become a professional balloonist straightaway.

Jane Woodville (31) – Divorced

Jane's interests included dance, travelling, herb-collecting and gardening. She had taken a Bi-lingual Secretarial Diploma and then Teaching English as a Foreign Language and subsequently got a job as a secretary in the oil industry. However, she disliked being unable to control her own working day and became increasingly frustrated. The break-down in her marriage only made matters worse.

Jane's assessment tests highlighted her need to be self-employed and the strong interest she had in alternative health regimes. She was advised to consider using these strengths to strike out on her own. After taking various suggested courses, she was able to set up a massage and healing practice aimed at stress-reduction through holistic therapy.

Anne Robson (22) – Single

Anne really had no idea what career she should follow. She took one year of a Diploma in Social Science and dropped out, only to find herself unemployed and directionless.

Anne's hobbies were very much centred on the performing arts: dancing, acrobatics, singing and acting, but she never believed she could make a career out of pursuing them. Based on her assessment tests, her careers adviser suggested she should take these interests far more seriously, particularly in the spheres of dance and movement. Anne took the advice, joined a Circus School and having secured jobs in touring companies was able to finally form her own group and tour abroad.

Nick Williams (42) – Single

In his late 20s, Nick began to find his career in computer sales and marketing less than fulfilling although he was doing well financially. He developed an interest in personal and spiritual development and while still employed began to give talks and workshops on some of his pet subjects, which he thoroughly enjoyed.

Over a period of three years he gradually decided this was

the way he wanted to go and gathered the courage and confidence to quit his corporate career. He started to make money from his new career and build up a reputation. He also began writing.

Nick now has an international business, a successful career as a coach and speaker and is generally much more fulfilled.

Nigel Elton (43) – Single

As a child, Nigel had always enjoyed dancing, movement and performing, but because he could never see a way of earning a living from it he became an accountant instead. He did well and was successful in this career but felt increasingly unfulfilled.

Seizing an opportunity, Nigel attended a training day with a clown and loved it so much he decided to take further training so he could perform as a clown himself. He took up freestyle dancing again and benefited from the movement therapy known as the Alexander technique.

Over time, Nigel was able to cut back on his job in accountancy and start practising as an Alexander teacher, perform as a clown and also teach dance. Whenever he needed any additional finance, he was still able to call on his accountancy experience to provide back up.

Steve Scott (35) – Divorced with two children

Steve worked for many years in the City of London as a finance manager and then became a housing control manager with a local authority. He never really enjoyed the way he earned his money.

Steve's hobbies had always been counselling and healing and he enjoyed visiting sacred places. He became a volunteer at a lecture series in London and began to realise he could carve a career for himself in ways that he enjoyed and fulfilled him.

Steve started training as a healer and began to practise, also organising retreats which proved highly successful, attracting great numbers of interested people. He then went on to give talks to groups both in the UK and abroad.

With his new-found confidence, Steve was able to offer his

previous organisational and management skills to another group he supported. In this way he was able to build up a portfolio which gave him a diverse means of earning a living which both stimulated and enriched him.

Glossary

British Psychological Society (BPS): the professional body for practising psychologists in Great Britain.

career guidance: see vocational guidance.

Career Development Loans (CDLs): funds managed by the Department for Education and Skills in partnership with a number of high street banks available to support a wide range of vocational courses.

Chartered Institute of Personnel and Development: the professional body for personnel and training officers in the UK and the Republic of Ireland.

curriculum vitae (CV): a resumé of personal details, interests and previous employment often requested *in lieu of* of an application form.

DfES: the central government Department for Education and Skills set up to provide an integrated approach to education and the aquisition of employment skills.

Disability Discrimination Act 1995 (DDA): an Act to prevent employers of 15 or more people from treating a disabled person less favourably than an able-bodied person unless there is a very good reason for doing so. Disability under the Act includes physical, sensory or mental disability as well as severe disfigurement.

distance learning: a variety of study methods which do not involve regular attendance at college.

employment tribunal: a quasi-judicial body set up to resolve employment rights disputes (previously known as an industrial tribunal).

Jobcentre: locally based government agency also known as Jobcentre Plus providing advice and guidance on jobs and an advertising service for job vacancies.

Learner Support Funds: funds made available by colleges to help students in financial difficulties.

Learning and Skills Councils (LSCs): 47 locally based organisations in England with responsibility for over 16s training provisions from April 2001.

learning curve: the line on a graph depicting the ability to learn in relation to age.

life skills: practical and social skills which contribute towards getting the best out of life.

means-testing: the calculation of the amount of assistance to be given or contribution made taking into account personal or family income offset by specific allowances.

motivational drives: aspects of personality which decide priorities in the desire to do one thing rather than another.

occupational psychologist: a trained practitioner in human behaviour who can advise on the best career to match individual skills, personality and motivational drives.

outplacement: an imported term from the USA meaning redundancy, usually involving active counselling by a firm of occupational psychologists.

The Peter Principle: the hypothesis that people are promoted to the job immediately above their level of competency.

portable skills: special talents or abilities which can be adapted or reshaped by an individual to suit different working environments.

proactive: taking the initiative rather than waiting for events to happen.

reactive: responding to events rather than taking the initiative.

redundancy: the loss of a job when this is no longer required by the employing company or organisation.

transferable skills: see **portable skills**.

tuition fees: the sum which a college or university charges to help meet the cost of teaching students on a course.

vocational guidance: professional advice on the most appropriate work to match personal qualities and skills.

Useful Addresses

The British Psychological Society
St Andrews House
48 Princess Road East
Leicester LE1 7DR
Tel: (0116) 254 9568
Fax: (0116) 247 0787
Email: mail@bps.org.uk

Career Analysts
Career House
90 Gloucester Place
London W1H 4BL
Tel: (020) 7935 5452
Fax: (020) 7486 9922
Email: info@careeranalysts.co.uk
www.careeranalysts.co.uk

The Scottish Executive Education Department
Victoria Quay
Edinburgh EH6 6QQ
Tel: (0131) 556 8400
Minicom: (0131) 244 1829
Email: ceu@scotland.gov.uk
Website: www.scotland.gov.uk

Scottish Executive Enterprise and Lifelong Learning
Department,
Meridian Court,
Cadogan Street,
Glasgow G2 6AT
Tel: (08457) 741 741
Website: www.scotland.gov.uk

Department of Employment and Learning in Northern Ireland,
    Adelaide House,
    39–49 Adelaide Street,
    Belfast BT2 8FD
    Tel: (028) 9025 7777
    Fax: (028) 9025 7778
    Website: www.delni.gov.uk

Department for Education and Lifelong Learning
    National Assembly for Wales
    Cardiff Bay
    Cardiff CF99 1NA
    Tel: (029) 2082 5111
    Website: www.wales.gov.uk

The Open and Distance Learning Quality Council
    16 Park Crescent
    London W1B 1AH
    Tel: (020) 7612 7090
    Fax: (020) 7612 7092
    Email: info@odlqc.org.uk
    Website: www.odlqc.org.uk

The Open University
    Walton Hall
    Milton Keynes
    MK7 6AA
    Tel: (01908) 274066
    Fax: (01908) 653744
    Website: www.open.ac.uk

Educational Grants Advisory Service
    The Family Welfare Association
    501–505 Kingsland Road
    Dalston
    London E8 4AU
    Tel: (020) 7254 6251
    Website: www.egas-online.org

Further Reading

An A-Z of Careers and Jobs, Diane Burston (Kogan Page, 8th edition)

Assertiveness, Gillen (CIPD)

The Book of Career Questions, Max Eggert (Trotman)

Be Prepared! Getting Ready for Job Interviews, Julie-Ann Amos (How To Books)

Build Your Own Rainbow, Barrie Hopson and Mike Scally (Management Books 2000)

Career Change, Ruth Lancashire and Roger Holdsworth (Hobsons)

Careers Encyclopedia, Audrey Segal (Cassell, 14th edition)

A Careers Guide for Adults, Margaret Korving (Trotman)

Effective Learning, Alan Mumford (CIPD)

Getting the Right Job, Judy Skeats (Ward Lock)

Go it Alone: the streetwise secrets of self-employment, Geoff Burch (Thorsons)

Handling Tough Job Interviews, Julie-Ann Amos (How To Books, 2nd edition)

How to Choose a Career, Vivien Donald (Kogan Page)

Independent Careers, edited by Klaus Boehm and Jenny Lees-Spalding (Bloomsbury)

Know Your Own Personality, Glen Wilson and H. J. Eysenck (Penguin)

Manage Your Own Career, Ben Ball (British Psychological Society and Kogan Page)

The Mid Career Action Guide, Derek and Fred Kemp (Kogan Page)

Offbeat Careers: *Sixty ways to avoid becoming an accountant*, Vivien Donald (Kogan Page)

Passing Psychometric Tests, Andrea Shavick (How To Books)

Penguin Careers Guide, Anna Alston and Anne Daniel (Penguin, 10th edition)

Rate Yourself!, Marthe Sansregret and Dyanen Adams (Kogan Page)

Successful Interviews Every Time, Dr Rob Yeung (How To Books, 2nd edition)

Telephone Skills, Forsyth (CIPD)

Test your Aptitude and Ability, Gareth Lewis (Hodder & Stoughton)

Test your Personality, Gene Crozier (Hodder & Stoughton)

What Colour is your Parachute?, Richard Nelson Bolles (Ten Speed Press)

The Work We Were Born To Do, Nick Williams (Element)

Index

159

If you want to know how ... to be headhunted

'This book is intended to meet a pressing need. Every day, large numbers of people contact executive search firms in the hope of finding a job or a non-executive directorship. Many of them do so without fully understanding the business of headhunting. We looked for a book to help such candidates, without success – and therefore decided to write one of our own.'

John Purkiss & Barbara Edlmair

How to be Headhunted
The insider's guide to making executive search work for you

John Purkiss & Barbara Edlmair

If your looking for a senior executive position – or a seat on the board – this book will tell you what you need to know.

- Learn about the search industry and the prominent firms within it
- Understand the recruitment process and make it work to your advantage
- Prepare a persuasive covering letter and a 'head-hunter-friendly' CV

Headhunting has long been shrouded in mystique. This book is the insider's guide, packed with practical tips to help you approach executive search firms.

ISBN 1 85703 996 3

If you want to know how ... to prepare for interviews

'It's the interviewer's prerogative to throw just about any question they can think of at the interviewee. So you might think that it's almost impossible to prepare for an interview. But the truth is that 80% of interview questions revolve around 20 common themes. And many interviewees let themselves down by not thinking about these themes, preparing and rehearsing responses to them.

'Many candidates then go on to create a wrong impression. Remember that an interviewer has to *like* you and warm to you as a person, as well as want to work with you because you answer the questions well. I see too many candidates who talk too much or come across as nervous or unfriendly. If you get the chance to rehearse with a friend and get some feedback on just how you come across, you will improve your chances no end.'

Rob Yeung

Successful Interviews – Every Time

Rob Yeung

'Successful Interviews is the type of book that one may not wish to share with others who are job seeking in competition with oneself. Nevertheless, I owe a debt of gratitude to Dr Rob Yeung for sharing his experiences with us ...' – *S. Lewis, Coventry*

'This book is an invaluable source of information for job hunters on preparing for interviews, tests and assessment centres.' – Jonathan Turpin, Chief Executive of job hunting *website fish4jobs.co.uk*

ISBN 1 85703 978 5

If you want to know how ... to pass psychometric tests

Over 95% of FTSE 100 companies use psychometric testing to
select their staff; as do the police, the Civil Service, local
authorities, the Armed Forces, the Fire Service, financial
institutions, retail companies, the communications industry, the
motor industry, the power industry – the list is endless. In fact, the
vast majority of large–medium sized organisations use psychometric
tests to recruit. So if you're looking for a job you need to know
what to expect. This book gives you the information, confidence
and practice to do that, and more.

Passing Psychometric Tests
Know what to expect and get the job you want

Andrea Shavick

'An insightful book.' – *The Guardian*

'A very good aid for those who might find themselves facing a
psychometric questionnaire.' – *Irish Examiner*

ISBN 1 85703 819 3

How To Books are available through all good bookshops, or you can order direct from us through Grantham Book Services.

Tel: +44 (0)1476 541080
Fax: +44 (0)1476 541061
Email: orders@gbs.tbs-ltd.co.uk

Or via our website

www.howtobooks.co.uk

To order via any of these methods please quote the title(s) of the book(s) and your credit card number together with its expiry date.

For further information about our books and catalogue, please contact:

How To Books
3 Newtec Place
Magdalen Road
Oxford OX4 1RE

Visit our web site at

www.howtobooks.co.uk

Or you can contact us by email at info@howtobooks.co.uk

Contents

By the same author
The Job Application Handbook
Passing That Interview

Published by How To Books Ltd,
3 Newtec Place, Magdalen Road,
Oxford OX4 1RE, United Kingdom
Tel: (01865) 793806   Fax: (01865) 248780

Third edition (revised and updated) 1999
Fourth edition 2002
Fifth edition 2004
Sixth edition 2006

British Library Cataloguing in Publication Data
A catalogue record for this book is available from
the British Library

Cover design by Baseline Arts Ltd, Oxford
Produced for How To Books by Deer Park Productions, Tavistock
Typeset by Anneset Productions, Weston-super-Mare, Somerset
Printed and bound by Cromwell Press, Trowbridge, Wiltshire

NOTE: The material contained in this book is set out in good
faith for general guidance and no liability can be accepted
for loss or expense incurred as a result of relying in particular
circumstances on statements made in the book. The laws and
regulations are complex and liable to change, and readers should
check the current position with the relevant authorities before
making personal arrangements.

SIXTH EDITION: *Thoroughly revised and updated reference section*

PLANNING A
CAREER
CHANGE

JUDITH
JOHNSTONE

howtobooks

If you want to know how . . .

Passing That Interview
Your step-by-step guide to coming out on top

Handling Tough Job Interviews
Be prepared, perform well, get the job

Turn Redundancy to Opportunity
Proven techniques and programmes for taking charge of your future

Returning to Work
A guide to re-entering the job market

Please send for a free copy of the latest catalogue to:

How To Books
3 Newtec Place,
Magdalen Road,
Oxford OX4 1RE,
United Kingdom
email: info@howtobooks.co.uk
www.howtobooks.co.uk

PLANNING A
CAREER
CHANGE